T0361619

Hey Dad...

Hey Dad...

Everything You Should've Learned About Life (But Didn't).

ROB FINLAY

Author of the *Wall Street Journal* Bestselling
Beyond the Building

A POST HILL PRESS BOOK
ISBN: 979-8-89565-088-2
ISBN (eBook): 979-8-89565-089-9

This book, as well as any other Post Hill Press publications, may be purchased in bulk quantities at a special discounted rate. Contact orders@posthillpress.com for more information.

This is a work of nonfiction. All people, locations, events, and situations are portrayed to the best of the author's memory.

Post Hill Press
New York • Nashville
posthillpress.com

Published in the United States of America
1 2 3 4 5 6 7 8 9 10

To all the dads, moms, step-parents, grandparents, guardians, mentors, and anyone who steps up to guide the next generation.

This book is dedicated to you. Your wisdom, patience, and care create the foundation on which others stand. You offer advice, not to impose a path, but to shine a light so that those you love can find their own way. Whether through late-night calls, quiet conversations, or just leading by example, your presence shapes the future in ways big and small. Thank you for helping us grow, learn, and face the world with courage and confidence. This book would not exist without you.

ACKNOWLEDGMENTS

I would like to extend my heartfelt thanks to everyone who contributed to making this book possible. First and foremost, to the contributors who generously shared their time and insights—your input is invaluable, and your names are listed below.

Dr. Lisa Miller
Brittany Canaski
Natalie Fisher
Lou Adler
Barry Moltz
Jayson Siu
DeShena Woodard
Matt Gromada
Mark Steber
Rod Griffin
Ryan Viktorin
Toni Eubanks
Charlie Nebe
Mark Flockhart
Niki McNeill Brown
Jeff Thorman

Melissa Maker
Ray and Zach Shefska
Mike McDowell
Travis Peterson
Jason Kelley
Jacqueline Whitmore
Thomas Farley
Robert Gressis
Doug Barnard
Scott Keyes
Joel Lambert
William Van Tassel, PhD
Jack Raia

I am deeply grateful to my incredible team: Jenn Locke, Dan Monfried, Amanda Kuehl, and Michael Yates for their dedication and hard work. Special thanks to my mom, Carroll, and my mother-in-law, Polly, for their thoughtful comments and edits.

Lastly, my deepest appreciation goes to my wife, Aynsley, who has listened to her fair share of "Hey Dad" calls, which sparked the idea for this book. And of course, none of this would have been possible without my wonderful kids, RJ, Maggie, Morgan, and Christa, and their dynamic role in content creation. Their support and inspiration have been instrumental in bringing this project to life.

Thank you all.

TABLE OF CONTENTS

INTRODUCTION

The buzz of my cell phone woke me at one in the morning. When I saw my daughter's name flash across the screen, my heart skipped a beat as I snatched the phone from the nightstand.

"Hey, Dad?"

I held my breath. A phone call in the middle of the night is the thing parents fear most.

"What's wrong?"

"I'm fine."

I let out my breath. "What is it, then?"

"We're at a gas station and they're all out of gas except for the green kind. Can I put that in my Jeep?"

"The…green kind?"

Relieved and groggy, I tried to make sense of what my daughter was asking.

My daughter and her friends were on a road trip. They'd traveled from Wisconsin to Austin and were now en route to Charlotte. The aim of this road trip: to scout cities from which they might launch their post-college lives. My daughter was on an adventure. I watched from the sidelines, filled with pride. I'd determined I would step on the playing field of her life when she asked me, and only then; the ball game was now hers. Now I was being called onto the field. Put me in, Coach.

The green kind.

It was May 2021, and much of the East Coast had been affected by a ransomware attack on the Colonial Pipeline. Lots of stations had no gas, period. What they *did* have was—

"You know, Dad. The kind with the green handle?"

"Do you mean *diesel?*"

"Yeah, I guess so." My daughter huffed. "So can I put that in the Jeep?"

And that's when I realized something: I'd failed my daughter. Well, not just her. I'd failed all four of my kids.

Maybe I'm being dramatic. Failure is relative, after all. Yet that's the thought I had in the middle of that May night— *Clearly, I've failed my kids if they wake me from a perfectly good sleep to ask if they can put diesel in a gas engine.* I'd skipped this lesson in the curriculum of "How to Be an Adult."

What else had I missed?

This book is my attempt to cover my bases. To go back into the curriculum and fill in the holes, to teach the things I wish I'd gotten ahead of when my kids were still under my roof.

Three or four times a week, I get these calls: "Hey, Dad, how do I...?" Fill in the blank: How do I get a car loan? Check a circuit breaker in my apartment? Know when to change my oil? I'm like Siri, an on-call genie who's supposed to have all the answers. I'll tell you right now: *I don't have all the answers.* But, I have learned certain things which will shorten your learning curve and make for an easier transition out of the secondary and post-secondary education system into the uncharted worlds of being "grown:" first jobs, first apartment, first move away from home, and so on. That's the goal of this book: to shorten the learning curve. Until now, you probably haven't had to think about all the Adulting "firsts" too much. You may have gone from your parents' home straight to college: each season brought with it a new curriculum to master on the way to earning your degrees. Once you graduate, the curriculum is loose and never-ending. Welcome to Adulthood.

If you're reading this book, you're probably in one of two categories:

1. Just graduated college or high school.

Graduating college is a major accomplishment...that can also feel like stepping off a cliff. What comes now? What are you supposed to do *next*? And *when*? Maybe, like my kids, you call a parent or other mentor figure for advice two to three (or twenty-three) times a week. Consider this your "Adulting" handbook. Maybe the material here will save you some stressed-out, middle-of-the-night phone calls that nearly give your loved ones a heart attack. I'm not covering every facet of adulthood here, but I'm doing my best to go broad. Are you attending your first business dinner soon? What do all those numbers on your tires mean? And why is having good credit such a big deal, anyway? We'll cover all of those topics here—and much, much more. Think of this book as your first call: rather than speed-dialing your emergency contact or watching five hours of YouTube tutorials, you can flip to the appropriate section in this book for a primer on how to handle each new adulting scenario.

And for the high school grads: statistics show that 62 percent of high school graduates go on to college,[1] which means 38

---

1   "61.4 percent of recent high school graduates enrolled in college in October 2023," U.S. Bureau of Labor Statistics, May 10, 2024, https://www.bls.gov/opub/ted/2024/61-4-percent-of-recent-high-school-graduates-enrolled-in-college-in-october-2023.htm#:~:text=Of%20the%203.1%20million%20people,in%20October%20of%20that%20year.

percent do not. If you're a recent high school graduate you could be on a different adulting track: preparing for trade school, the military, or jumping into entrepreneurship. Whether you're a recent grad preparing for more school or jumping with both feet into the world of work, this book is for you. Adulting doesn't begin when you're twenty-two and end when you're twenty-five; nor does it begin at eighteen and end at twenty-two. Adulting happens as you move from dependence on someone else to independence...and it never ends. That could be seen as bad news, but I hope you see it as good news. There's nothing to master here. We're in this together.

2. Parent, grandparent, or relative of a high school or college grad.

Perhaps you gave this book as a gift to a young adult in your life. Perhaps (like me) you find yourself in a strange position: kids calling you at all hours for various "How do I's...?" while simultaneously disregarding every unasked-for piece of advice.

I get it. Often, my kids are more prone to hear something if it doesn't come from me. Fortunately for us, I got to interview certified experts for this book. I did this on the theory that if my kids won't take my word for it—whatever the "it" may be—they'll take the word of an expert they're not related to. For each chapter of this book, I spoke to experts in fields ranging from credit card point travel to apartment leasing. Advice from these experts forms the backbone of this book, along with the good old-fashioned common sense we hope our kids pick up somewhere along the way. This book is another tool that can serve as another waypoint in their journey.

HOW TO USE THIS BOOK

Along with the text in each section of this book, there are accompanying YouTube and TikTok videos. (Because I know how you're getting most of your information!) Each section contains an interview with an expert in the particular area discussed in that chapter. I've talked to a wide range of experts, from CEOs to mechanics. I've highlighted the top tips they offered; at the end of each chapter, there's a TL;DR (too long; didn't read) list so you'll get the highlights of the highlights. My hope is that you'll feel more secure in your "adulting" efforts after reading each chapter. I want this book to be something you refer back to often, like a manual; let this book be something you *use*. I want you to know that as you're going out into the world and experiencing all of the "firsts" coming your way, you can stand on your own two feet. You're making your way. No one ever does it alone; when you need extra support, this book will be there for you—perhaps closer than a phone call to your parents. (Though they'll be there for you, too. And by the way, you should call them—they want to hear your voice. Just not at one in the morning.)

Believe it or not, adulting doesn't have to be scary. It can feel good—cozy, even, like putting on comfy clothes and watching football. Things that seem mystifying right now—like pulling a credit report and setting up the utilities on your first apartment—will eventually become old hat. You'll get good at handling the routine, banal aspects of everyday life so that you can free up energy to focus on the *big* questions: What do I like to do? What contribution can I make? Which path is most likely to lead to a happy, purposeful life?

Here's some more good news: *You don't have to know the answer to these questions right now.* Or ten years from now. This is the nature of young adulthood: You pick one track, try it out, and then you pick again. You make slight adjustments along the path you've chosen. At this time in your life, you can pivot and change course with little consequence. That's fantastic! While this book won't help you figure out what to do with your life, it *will* help you become the adult who can face that question again and again, taking action as you discover more about what lights you up. That's all part of growing up: facing the big questions with courage and a fully rooted sense of self.

I can tell you how to prepare for a job interview: I *can't* tell you which career path will bring you the most meaning and fulfillment. Unfortunately, neither can your parents or Google or social media. But in the same way I do for my own kids and your loved ones do for you, I can cheer you on and encourage you to play big—to not hold yourself back for fear you won't be able to handle the success you're destined for. You've got this. You are becoming the adult—the person—who can handle your life. Bring to the table all your curiosity, hard work, and joy; let life surprise you as it unfolds and prepare for adventure.

Your folks and I are cheering from the sidelines.

CHAPTER 1

GET A PLAN

How to decide what you want

I chose my first college based on the application process: fill out a postcard.

That was it. There was no SAT or ACT score needed, no essay requirement, no interview process—just a postcard to fill out and send to the College of Boca Raton in Florida. I filled out the postcard and got in.

Cue sigh of relief. I was thankful I'd found someplace to continue my learning because I wasn't a strong student. After high school I had three choices: (1) Get a job. (2) Join the Marine Corps. (3) Go to college.

My brother was in the Marine Corps; watching him, I saw I didn't have what it takes to make it as a Marine. Yet my grades weren't such that colleges were clamoring over me. Enter the College of Boca Raton and its postcard application. That fall after graduating high school, I packed up and headed from New Hampshire down to Florida.

I had only fuzzy ideas of what I wanted to do when I grew up—dreams and interests, but no plan. I knew I liked finance.

My dad had given me *Barron's Dictionary of Finance and Investment Terms*—no bigger than an iPhone, but thick. I loved to go through that little blue book and study the terms, imprinting the definitions of words like *compounding* and *hedging* in my brain. Plus, it was the '80s, and the movie *Wall Street* with Michael Douglas was big. Working on Wall Street became my dream: I wanted to be a trader in the big leagues, living in New York, immersed in the hustle and glamor and money of big finance.

Yet I was decidedly *not* on that track when I graduated high school. Young guys just out of college who landed plumb jobs on Wall Street were coming from Ivy League schools and fancy MBA programs, and that wasn't me. But I had to start somewhere, and Boca Raton let me in. I packed up my bags and left New Hampshire.

And then I came crawling right back.

I only lasted at the College of Boca Raton for a semester. Grade-wise, I hadn't gotten myself together—yet I didn't want to get a job, and I didn't want to go to the Marine Corps. I needed a Plan B.

I headed back to New Hampshire and contacted an admissions officer named Michael DeBlasi from the school down the street, New Hampshire College. I leveled with him: "Mr. DeBlasi, if you give me a chance, I'll work hard and apply myself. I'll go to class and get the grades I need to stay here."

Michael gave me the chance I needed. He let me into New Hampshire College and said that if I got Bs or better, I could stay. For the rest of college, I did. I lived at home, worked, and studied. I didn't join a fraternity or go to parties. I put my nose down and worked until graduation. Eventually, I *did* make it to

Wall Street—and discovered it was not all it was cracked up to be. But that's a story for later in the book and not the point of this chapter.

Here's the point: it's okay not to know what your life will look like. (But it's useful to have an idea of what you *don't* want your life to look like.)

Maybe you're reading this right after high school graduation. You know what college you're attending, or you're planning on trade school, the military, or some other path instead. Perhaps you're in college, nearing graduation and preparing to enter the "real world." Or maybe you're a newly minted college graduate about to enter the workforce or start your own business. At each new turn you may find yourself asking: Now what?

That question can be scary. Understandably so, because it's probably not one you've had to ask before. From kindergarten to twelfth grade, the path is laid out. You move along it like you're being carried by one of those moving sidewalks at the airport—automatically, without having to think too much. For most people, the moving sidewalk carries them into college. But after four years, the sidewalk drops you off.

If you're reading this, you've stepped off the sidewalk or are preparing to. Now what?

PREPARING FOR LIFE AFTER SCHOOL

This book is primarily for those young adults who are about to enter the working world. But if you're a young adult preparing for another big transition (such as high school to college, high school to military, and so on) I hope you'll find value here, too. Not everyone will, or *should*, take the same path. There is no one right path. In fact, there are as many different "right" paths as there are people in the world. And your path may not be entirely up to you—at least, not yet.

If you come from a strong military background, for instance, you may be encouraged to join the service. Maybe you're preparing for grad school in a particular program, but only because your folks have agreed to bankroll that degree. If you're a first-generation college student, you're charting a new path. A college education was never a given, and you've faced resistance as you've broken the mold.

Maybe you've been carrying the load of other people's expectations for a long time. Maybe you still are. Parental expectations and guardrails can limit you, but they can also provide useful direction as you start your path. You can carry those expectations for only so long, though. Eventually, you've got to ask yourself: What's important to *you*? What would make your life meaningful and exciting? If you were to nail down a vision and take one tiny step in that direction...what would it be?

THREE QUESTIONS TO ASK YOURSELF

Think of life like planning a hike. You choose the terrain (flat, rocky, rolling hills, steep inclines) and what you'd like to see (oceans, forests, rivers, etc.). Yet even though you get autonomy in choosing your hike, you can't know everything you'll see on the journey. The way may be more challenging than you'd imagined—or more beautiful. You may start traveling through a canyon, then midway through change your mind: you'd rather have an ocean view. So, you double back and start a new course. You haven't lost anything by first taking the canyon trek. Each path you travel adds to your experience and deepens your perspective. As you're starting your hike, consider: What kind of trek sounds the most interesting and exciting?

Here's a three-question framework for determining which kind of trail to set out on as you begin your hike:

1. What are my interests?

For me, I knew I was interested in finance. Wall Street was a faraway dream that I eventually achieved. Yet the journey from point A to point B was not linear: there were a few waypoints in between graduating with my degree in finance and economics (I stuck it out at the New Hampshire College after all) and landing a job on Wall Street.

That little blue book of financial terms was my anchor. Even though most of what I learned in school didn't interest me, I knew I could work hard on the things that *did* interest me. I always had a job. My parents ran their own business; I had their example of hard work to look up to. As a young adult trying to figure out my career, I didn't have a lot to go on except for the knowledge that finance excited me. That was enough to land me my first job. (That and a *lot* of resumes and cover letters mailed out, snail-mail style, to employers all over the country—plus a lot of hustling and getting hiring managers on the phone. But we'll talk about that later, too.)

What are your interests? What sparks your curiosity? Look back over your life and school career and follow the breadcrumbs. What did you love to learn about in school? What did you stay up late at night doing?

Let's say you're into art and always enjoyed playing around with graphic design. Maybe you even have a graphic design degree in hand. Believe it or not, that information is enough to get you started. What opportunities in graphic design can you find that look interesting?

Pick one and *go*. You can pivot and adjust later.

2. Who can help me move toward my interests?

To this day I'm still friends with Michael, the admissions officer who gave me my chance at New Hampshire College. I got a college education because he took a chance on me. As you're plotting your next move, look for those who are a few steps ahead. Who's where you think you want to be? How can you connect with that person and get closer to where you want to go? Remember: not knowing where you want to be is okay. Yet the more you network and talk to people who are ahead of you, the sooner you'll figure things out.

Networking is not about impressing anyone with your perfect grades, college transcript, list of extracurricular activities, et cetera. It's about being truthful—assessing where you are versus where you'd like to be—asking for help and offering help whenever you can. Case in point: how I had to level with Michael after my lackluster stint in Florida. There was no point in trying to impress him.

To meaningfully connect with people who can give you access to exciting opportunities, you must drop the "student/teacher" mindset. Throughout school and college, your teachers are the ones who set the rules for you to follow. They're the ones with the answers: you show up and do as you're told. Real life doesn't work that way.

Outside of school, other adults are your colleagues. They're your resources. They have things that you need—and *you* have things that *they* need. When you know how to connect with people, it doesn't matter what you do or how many times you pivot; you have what you need to get ahead. Remember that you never have to go it alone.

3. How can I test the waters?

Once you identify a direction and someone who can help you get there, *move*. Pick a swim lane and start swimming as soon as possible. If you love it, great. If you hate it, that's good information also. At least you haven't wasted too much time on the side of the pool, wondering how the water feels. Inaction and overthinking will be your worst enemies; don't give in to them. Just do something.

There's no sense in holding out for the perfect opportunity or the perfect job. You can't know what you like until you get in there and try *something*. If you get an opportunity that you're unsure about, go ahead and say yes (unless there are too many glaring red flags, such as a verbally abusive hiring manager or company practices that go against your core values). Say yes and figure it out later. You don't have to stay in a job forever. You *do* have to get started, though.

I've seen a lot of young people—including my kids—get twisted into knots about choosing the "right" thing. It's understandable: as a young person, you're making big decisions on your own for the first time. Everything feels like it's life or death. Trust me: *it's not*.

Are you afraid of making mistakes? I'll go ahead and let you off the hook—you're *bound* to make mistakes. Hundreds of mistakes. Big ones, small ones. But here's great news: you can afford to make them. You're not yet responsible for a family. Other people's well-being isn't on the line if you accidentally buy a crappy car, for example, or if you quit your job without thinking it through.

Take advantage of this time when you're nimble and can take risks. Worry less about making a five-year plan and more about making a move—*any* move—in the direction of your interests.

To gain more insights on how to find your ideal career, I spoke with Brittany Canaski and asked her how young adults can choose a path. Brittany is a life and leadership coach who's helped hundreds of people navigate their lives and careers the founder of the company Hello Velocity. I also spoke with Dr. Lisa Miller, a PhD and professor in the clinical psychology program at Teachers College, Columbia University, who is known for her breakthrough study on the importance of spirituality. She's also the bestselling author of *The Awakened Brain*, in which she explores the science of spirituality and how individuals can access spirituality to build lives of meaning and connection. Here's what Brittany and Dr. Miller had to say:

1. **Visualize a day in your life.**

    When considering different college majors, Brittany used visualization to rule out two career paths that sounded good on paper: doctor (too much blood, too much school) and hospitality (too many late nights and grumpy customers). When she thought about what she wanted her working life to look like, Brittany saw herself working a corporate, nine-to-five, high-paying job—so she began pursuing that path with a business degree. She stayed on it until the path was no longer exciting for her, years into her career, and then she decided to do something entirely different. (Remember that you can always change directions, but you must start walking.)

You can use visualization to rule out certain career paths and to hone your vision for your ideal future. If it were up to you, what would your day look like? Close your eyes. Imagine what you'd wear, what you'd do, whether or not you'd spend time outside, what kind of people you'd work with…see what comes up and let yourself be surprised.

2. **It's okay to go "shopping" for your career.**

Dr. Miller spent years exploring different career paths. She said this time of "research and development" (R&D), or "shopping," for her career was incredibly useful. As an emerging adult who doesn't yet have dependents, you can take your time choosing your path. She said it may take two years—or even more—to land in the career you feel passionate about.

Dr. Miller said the years she spent trying different professions (mediator, investment banker, working in an emergency room) was one of the most productive, important periods of her life. When she settled into her career as a scientist, she felt fully committed to it; she still loves her work today in her fifties as much as she did in her twenties. Science was "it" for Dr. Miller; she was willing to do what it took to progress in the field, and the things she was studying kept and held her interest.

You're not married to any job or career. Shopping for the right one may be the most important thing you do for yourself. Don't be afraid to explore.

3. **Don't worry about your peers—stay in your lane.**

When Brittany Canaski graduated from Cornell University and got her first role in the corporate world, she was making $55,000 a year. She thought that was great—until she learned that several of her business-degree peers landed jobs paying over $100,000 a year. But then, Brittany looked at their lives. They worked in finance and were often working eighty to a hundred hours a week. Brittany realized she didn't want that kind of stress and began to appreciate her salary and work-life balance even more.

Figuring out what you want from life and a career is an inside job. If you're struggling to make a move or identify what you want, get the help of a neutral third party (maybe a coach)—*don't* look to social media or worry about how you stack up against your friends. Other people's jobs and salaries may be data points for you to consider, but they're not enough to guide you. Take everything you see on social media with a grain (or a gallon) of salt and focus on living *your* real life—not on the social media version of your life.

4. **Listen to the Universe.**

A yoga class led Brittany to her first life coach. Brittany was fascinated by the way the yoga teacher spoke—it was unlike anything she'd heard before and she had to learn more.

Dr. Lisa Miller would call Brittany's experience in yoga class "listening to the Universe." It's a stance of living life with open eyes and ears and paying attention to the things that grab you. Tuning into guidance and figuring out your next step is something you'll do for the rest of your life—when deciding whom to marry, whether or not to have kids, whether to have *another* kid, whether to change jobs, whether to sell the house and buy an RV and travel the country…you get the picture. Life will always give you opportunities to pivot and adjust. If you're paying attention, you'll recognize the signs that it's time to make a change before they slap you in the face. If you learn to listen to the Universe now, you'll save yourself a lot of heartache (and maybe a mid-life crisis) later on.

HOW TO BECOME INDEPENDENT

I'll be upfront: I have an agenda for you. It's that you move out of your parents' or caregivers' house and be able to support yourself. I'm a dad, so naturally this is a selfish agenda: I don't want to pay for my kids forever. You may not share this agenda yet. You may get along great with your folks and have a cushy setup being a "stay at home" son or daughter, with millions of followers on social media and no need to earn your own money. If that's your deal…far be it from me to talk you out of a living situation where you're happy and rent-free.

Yet eventually, you'll want to move away. (I'm guessing your future spouse doesn't want to live with their in-laws.) If you're living with your parents right now, how can you strategically use the money you're saving to set yourself up for a solid financial future? You could pay down student loans faster, or save up for an investment like grad school, a real estate property, or the startup capital for your own business.

My point is, if you're living with your parents or another older adult, I hope you're doing so with an endgame in mind. For their sakes, but really for yours. I want you to have the confidence that comes from standing on your own two feet. That's what this book is meant to do.

For most of you, the first agenda item after graduation is "get a job," so that's the next chapter of this book. We'll cover how to find jobs that interest you, how to stand out in a sea of applications, how to interview well, and how to follow up after the interview and leave a strong impression. If you're interested in starting your own business, we'll talk about that in chapter 3. Chapter 4 is about managing your money. We'll talk about making sure your basic needs are met and how to budget for groceries, housing, car payments, and other necessities. In chapter 5, we'll explore how to financially set yourself up for the future by having good credit, saving, and investing.

Chapter 6 is all about how to find your own apartment—what to look for in a lease, how to research potential neighborhoods, what expenses you can expect outside of a lease, what to do if you need to get out of a lease, and so on. In chapter 7, you'll learn how to care for (furnish, clean, and do basic maintenance on) your place. Chapter 8 is all about cars: how to research them based on what's important to you, what to expect when you buy your first car, standard maintenance to stay on top of, and buying car insurance. In chapter 9 we'll look at "Everyday Manners and Adulting," a.k.a. "How Not to Be a Rude Slob." (Just kidding. Kind of.) We'll discuss things like when to send thank-you notes, how and whom to tip, and how often you should wash your sheets. Chapter 10 is all about travel: when to get the best deals on plane rides, what to do if you miss your flight, how to (safely) drink the water in developing countries, and more. Finally, in chapter 11 we'll cover the "oh, crap" situations in life, as in "My power steering is breaking down and I'm on the highway—oh, crap! What now?" Or "I've had this weird pain in my side for twelve hours and I can't stand up, but I don't have a primary care physician—oh crap!"

There's a throughline through all the sections you'll read. It's this: adulting is hard. Even those of us who've been doing it for a long time think so. No one is born knowing this stuff. If you make mistakes or have to learn a few things the hard way, don't beat yourself up: learn the lesson and do better next time. No one has got every aspect of adulting down, but we all get better over time.

THE "HEY, DAD" PARTING SHOTS

College admissions have a season. But when it comes to getting a job, pivoting in your career, and finding your calling, it's open admissions…for the rest of your life. It's up to you to reflect and go after what you want.

TL;DR

Here are the "too long, didn't read" bullet points for everything we covered in this chapter:

- Three questions to get you closer to your best-fit life path: (1) What are my interests? (2) Who can help me? And (3) How do I test those interests?
- Visualize a day in your future life. See what feels good and what feels like a "heck, no."
- "Go shopping" for your career. Try a lot of things. You've got time.
- Don't worry about your peers or how your life appears on social media. Live the *real* version of your life.
- Listen to the Universe. Guidance can come from unexpected places.

REFLECTION QUESTIONS

Even if you know your next move after graduation, take a moment to reflect on these questions and consider where you want to go long-term. I recommend writing your answers in a journal. Remember—you don't have to know the answers to these questions, and there's no way to get them "wrong." Just give them your best guess. (That's all any of us are ever doing!)

1. What's your long-term goal for your life? Identify three. (Examples: Own a business, write a book, live near the beach, start a family, travel the world, etc.)
2. What would you like to be doing six months from now? One year from now? Five years from now? Ten?
3. Where would you like to live? (Mountains, city, near the beach, etc.)
4. What do you imagine your future relationship situation to be? (e.g. Are you married? Do you have kids?)

5. Think back on the work you've done up to this point, either in school, a part-time job, or some other capacity. What work was the most meaningful to you? Why?

6. Is there someone you admire, either because of the career they have or the type of life they live, whom you'd like to grow closer to in the next phase of your life? Who?

7. (If you've got someone in mind, don't waste time; contact them and ask if you can take them to coffee sometime.)

CHAPTER 2

GET A JOB

How to hustle for the role you want

"**H**ello, my name is Rob Finlay and I'm a recent finance major college graduate. Is there any advice you can give me as I begin my career?"

I'd lost count of how many times I'd recited the script. I began making these calls to potential employers in the spring of '92, my last semester of college. This was before the internet. To even *get* on the phone with someone, I had to (1) look up the company's address in the phone book or book of lists, (2) print a paper resume and cover letter, tailored to each individual employer, and (3) mail it. I wore out a lot of printers. After all that, I'd call. And I didn't want to speak to just anyone; my goal was to go past human resources and get department heads who could actually *hire* me on the phone. I did this five hundred times.

Yes, you read that right: *five hundred times.* Where's a LinkedIn "Easy Apply" button when you need it? The process was tedious, painstaking. All those resumes sent—most of them may as well have gone into a black hole. But some of them didn't.

When I got someone from the company on the phone, I did a fist pump. *Yes!* A real-live person to speak to—that was already a win, even if I didn't get the job. I knew I had to sell myself and my abilities, but I didn't want to be weird about it. I'd introduce myself and talk briefly about my degree and background. Then, the money line: "I'm looking to get into [fill in the blank: finance, lending, trading, banking]. Is there any advice you can give me as I begin my career?"

I didn't come out and ask for a job; though, the "recent college graduate" line was a giveaway. The first few times I had these conversations, I was nervous. The folks I was calling had important work and busy schedules, and I'd be lucky if they didn't chew me out—at least, that's what I thought. But that turned out not to be true. My overwhelming experience: people were friendly and more than willing to help a college kid with a little gumption. (There's a name for this phenomenon; it's called the Ben Franklin effect, and we'll get into it a little later.)

Finally, *finally*, I got an interview with Midlantic Bank in New Jersey. But an interview was not an offer, and I was interested in living in the South. I had another interview with a bank in Atlanta. Because I wanted to give life in the South a go, I loaded all of my worldly possessions into my old Mazda 929 with over two hundred thousand miles on it and headed south on I-95 toward Atlanta. I stayed at a La Quinta Inn on a week-to-week basis as I interviewed with the Atlanta bank and applied for other jobs. My chances were better at landing a job in Georgia if I was a resident, so I became one—albeit a resident slumming it at the La Quinta Inn.

Ultimately, things didn't work out in Atlanta, and I packed my car once again, headed up north, and began my career at Midlantic Bank in New Jersey.

Despite my inglorious career beginnings, I was proud to be working and making my own money. Thank goodness so much of job applying and interviewing is easier than it was back then. Today, you can tailor your resume and cover letter in an instant with ChatGPT; you can look up a company's organization chart on LinkedIn and get in touch with a hiring manager directly; you can stalk your preferred employers on social media and figure out what will make you attractive as an employee. You certainly don't have to kill as many trees as I did with my reams of printed resumes.

Yet there were lessons I learned as I put in the reps and eventually got my first job that are useful for you, even in today's vastly different landscape. No one will tell you that breaking into your first job and getting on the right career track *for you* are easy. Yet millions have done it before you. You may need to knock on a lot of doors. Getting your first job may require more work than you've ever done up to this point. But you're up for it.

When you're looking to break into your first job, here's a six-step framework for finding opportunities, getting hired, and wowing your employers:

1. Look for companies you would like to work for.

This one is pretty self-explanatory. Have you always dreamed of working in big tech at a FAANG (Facebook, Apple, Amazon, Netflix, Google) company? Or would you prefer to get your start in a small business so you can have a hand in every part of how the sausage gets made?

Think about what you would like the beginning of your career to look like. What experiences would you like to have?

What kind of people would you like to work with? Cast a wide net as you begin your search—then narrow it. The internet is great for looking for companies—but it's even better to talk to real people. If your university hosts job fairs, go. Check out the companies that are recruiting and see which ones you feel drawn toward. You may go in with an idea of what you like and come away completely surprised. It's best to approach this with an open mind.

I spoke with hiring expert Lou Adler and asked his advice on getting your first job. Lou is the CEO of The Adler Group, a consulting and training firm that helps companies hire talent, and the bestselling author of the books *Hire with Your Head* and *The Essential Guide for Hiring and Getting Hired*. Over the last three decades, he's helped over forty thousand recruiters make hiring decisions.

In our conversation, Lou recommended starting your job search close to home. He says to look for jobs hiring in your area and to see if they require your skillset. Lou also recommends taking advantage of job placement services offered by your university. There are people whose job it is to make sure *you* get a job once you graduate. *Use them.* Use everything you've got. If there's help available…take it!

2. Research the company via sites like Crunchbase, Glassdoor, and LinkedIn.

This is one area where you have a major advantage that I didn't have when I was starting out: the internet. There's a goldmine of information on your potential employers. In case you're not already using platforms like Crunchbase, Glassdoor, and LinkedIn, here's a primer on what each can do for your job search:

- **Crunchbase:** Crunchbase is a platform that provides information about businesses, including insider info like how much funding a startup received on their last venture capital round, who's in leadership, and other industry news. Investors use Crunchbase when determining what startups to fund. If you're interested in working for a startup and the inner workings of how companies get funded by venture capitalists, use this database as a research tool.

- **Glassdoor:** On Glassdoor, current and past employees of a company can review the company. Employees share, anonymously, their experience working for the business. They also share their pay: you can click on a job description and see the range of salaries offered for that position. This puts you in a great spot when you (eventually) interview for the company and need to have a grounded, realistic discussion about salary (more on this later).

  Take Glassdoor with a grain of salt, just like you would any review website. Some folks love to go on sites like Yelp, for instance, and blast a hamburger that dozens of other people are raving about. If you see an overly caustic review while the rest are milder, get curious. Are the reviews mostly positive? Consider that a green flag. And remember: no workplace is ever perfect.

- **LinkedIn:** You probably don't need me to tell you about LinkedIn. But just in case you do, it's a social media platform for businesses, job seekers, business owners, solopreneurs—everyone. Basically, it's the social media for work. LinkedIn is the easiest place to get information about a potential employer, connect with hiring managers and individuals working there, and build your personal brand (in other words, put out content that shows people who can hire you what you're all about).

Natalie Fisher, another job expert I spoke to, uses LinkedIn both to promote her company *and* to help her clients get jobs. Natalie runs a program called "Get a Six-Figure Job You Love." When she was traditionally employed, Natalie always found it easy to get jobs and promotions—something she credits to not having limiting beliefs about what was possible for her. When Natalie was laid off, she turned her attention to helping others harness an abundance mindset in their job search: she's now coached hundreds of people and helped them find fulfilling, lucrative careers. Using LinkedIn effectively is a great way to connect with those careers, according to Natalie.

Natalie advises her clients to connect directly with potential employers on the platform and to set up real-time conversations with them (more on how to do that and what to say later). When building your personal brand and posting content on LinkedIn, Natalie says to choose images and content that you'd be proud to share with your family. LinkedIn is a two-way street: it provides an opportunity for you to research employers and connect with people who can hire you, *and* for you to put out content that, like a Bat-Signal, draws those employers *to you*. The sooner you use this platform and get comfortable there, the better.

3. Network, network, network.

Perhaps the thought of calling hiring managers directly (like I did) or messaging them on LinkedIn makes you want to throw up. Maybe you've never been so forward about going after what you want. You've been in "student mode," where you let the teacher take the reins, do as you're told, and make good grades (or not, if you're me). It's time to break out of that mindset.

From here on out, you need to sell yourself. Employers—especially small business owners—like gumption. I know it may feel uncomfortable to get on a video call or pick up the phone and call someone. You're probably far more comfortable communicating via text. Yet if you can practice conversing with folks in real time, either on video calls or the phone, you stand out. If I get thirty emails a day but one person calls me, that person stands out. Even if it feels weird, you *can* get better at talking to employers and people in your ideal jobs and selling them on what you have to offer. The more you do it, the more natural it will feel.

If the word "sell" freaks you out, it doesn't have to. You don't have to be weird about it! Selling is about being direct, forthright, and honest. You have to sell yourself to get an interview, and then a job. You must sell yourself to get a promotion. If you start your own business, you'll need to sell yourself to potential clients to win their business. Selling yourself is about believing in what you have to offer (in this case, yourself) and showing your potential employer the value of what you bring to the table. It's about making real connections with people: knowing what their needs are, how you can help, and then offering that help. *You* are the missing ingredient a company is looking for—whether or not they know it. If you take initiative in this way (reaching out to potential employers and showing them value), you'll make a strong first impression…and first impressions are powerful.

Employers like boldness and hustle. Even though things have changed since I was first on the job hunt, the underlying ethos is the same: Hustle. Be professional and polite. *Own* your value and offer it generously. Follow up—the squeaky wheel gets the grease. Nervous? That's okay—practice being nervous and doing it anyway. Eventually, someone is going to be so glad you went to all that trouble. You're going to get hired and knock it out of the park for them. By selling yourself, you're *helping* them. Start making those connections and putting yourself out there.

Here's an interesting dynamic: people like you *more* after they've done a favor for you. Not after you've done a favor for *them*—after they've done a favor for *you*.

This is the Ben Franklin effect, and here is its origin story: Benjamin Franklin was at odds with a fellow legislator. He heard this legislator had a rare book in his library; Franklin asked to borrow it. The rival agreed. After a week, Franklin returned the book with a note about how much he liked it. After this exchange, the legislator changed his attitude toward Franklin; he was polite, suddenly willing to help in areas where the two men had previously butted heads. Franklin and the legislator grew to be good friends. Franklin wrote about it in his autobiography and penned this saying: "He that has once done you a kindness will be more ready to do you another, than he whom you yourself have obliged."

Put in plain English: If someone has done something nice for you, they're more likely to do something nice again. They like you even better than if you'd been the one to do the nice thing!

This is why I had such pleasant conversations with people when I was cold-calling employers. People want to help. You're not putting them out by asking for help—you're doing them a favor. Really!

Note: This phenomenon works if you have some kind of connection with the person you're asking for help. In Benjamin Franklin's case, he saw his rival in the legislature each day. In my case, I'd already sent the resumes and the cover letter to the places I wanted to work. My cards were on the table: everyone knew I wanted a job. I'm not talking about calling up random people and asking them to do you the "favor" of hiring you.

A story illustrates this point well: There was a young woman named Erin who got a job delivering beverages to people on the golf course. A "cart girl" job can be lucrative—it pays about $15 an hour, plus tips—but it's not a role people stay in long-term. Erin could have clocked in for work, done her time, and then clocked out—on to the next thing. Instead, she started talking to the people she was serving.

A golfer would talk about their business and their hiring needs. Erin had peers who had the skillsets the business owner was looking for; she would recommend her friends. Golfers began seeking Erin out; she became an unofficial recruiter for the golfers she was serving and for her peer group. In the meantime, Erin got numerous job offers from the people she delivered drinks to—and those jobs paid a lot more than "cart girl." All because she knew how to talk to people and help them (which is networking in a nutshell). Erin formed relationships with people on the golf course: when it was time to call in help for herself and land her next role, she had an army of supporters behind her.

Take a lesson from Erin and Ben Franklin: give people the chance to help you. Your age and inexperience are your biggest assets right now. Read that sentence again. By giving someone the chance to help you, you're giving them a gift. There's something extremely gratifying about helping a young person who's just starting out. So how do you make connections with folks who can then connect you with the right opportunities?

Repeat steps one and two: look for companies you'd like to work for, research them, and connect with people in hiring roles (*not* human resources) or with folks in the role you're after. Send a message or email that goes something like this: "Hello, my name is _____. I'm a recent college graduate [or soon-to-be graduate] with a degree in _____. I'm excited to begin my career in _____ and I admire your company because _____. Would you have fifteen to twenty minutes to tell me about your experience with the company?"

The more people you get involved in your job search, the more people you have invested in your success—and that can only be a good thing.

According to Lou Adler, networking isn't about connecting with people at random. Start where you are. Talk to folks you've worked with in the past or people who can highly recommend you and say: "Hey, I know we worked together last summer. Are there two or three people you can connect me with who I can meet?" Likely, the person you're asking will say "Sure—you did a great job for me, I'd be happy to help." They'll connect you with someone, who'll recommend someone *else* for you to connect with. You'll meet that new person: In the conversation, say, "Here's what I'm looking for, and here's what I'm really good at." And the person you're speaking to will connect you with someone else...and on and on it goes, until you get hired. This is the way it works. Lou says you have about a one in five hundred chance of getting the job via cold applying. A much more efficient route is to have fifteen networking conversations that yield three or four interviews.

Natalie Fisher also touts the benefits of networking. Natalie says that genuineness is an essential ingredient in networking. Express genuine interest in the person you're meeting: focus more on *them* than on sharing about yourself. Natalie's clients often secure job offers via their personal connections and the conversations they have with them. According to Natalie, it's best not to overthink these conversations if you're new to them: even short conversations in which you ask for career advice can lead to big opportunities. (Can you say Ben Franklin effect?)

I just gave a lot of airtime to networking. But that's because it's *the* most important thing you can do to get that first job, and then to progress in your career. But it's not only valuable for job hunting; networking will make your life richer and result in new friendships. Start now; commit to taking lots of imperfect action. Get comfortable talking with people. Remember—at the end of the day, that's all networking is.

4. Interview confidently.

Lou Adler says you should spend as much time preparing for an interview as you would for a presentation to the CEO. Prior to the interview, write down all your strengths and weaknesses.

Then, write out a story to go with each one. For example, don't just say you're good at collaborating: prove it with a story. For your weaknesses, share stories in which you address them honestly—and then say what you do to overcome them.

Lou has an acronym for answering interview questions: SAFW, or "say a few words." Make an opening statement. Then, your next sentence will amplify that opening statement. Your prepared story comes next: two to three sentences in which you illustrate for the interviewer a scenario in which this concept played out. For your final statement, wrap it up. According to Lou, one to one and a half minutes, two minutes tops, is the sweet spot for answering questions. Speak for less time and you run the risk of seeming unsure of yourself; speak longer than two minutes and you look arrogant.

In our conversation, Lou shared about one time in an interview when he got thrown an oddball question. The interviewer asked: "How would you market a lightbulb?" Lou said, "I gotta tell you, I don't have a clue. If you asked me how to manufacture and distribute light bulbs and figure out the cost, that's what I'm really good at. And I'm happy to describe it. I'm not great at marketing, but I'm really good at cost accounting and manufacturing." Lou got the job. If you get a wacky question, Lou says to push back—show the interviewer you can't be knocked around.

Natalie Fisher also stressed the importance of doing your homework ahead of an interview. In our conversation, Natalie recommended understanding the business's mission and values prior to the interview. Like Lou, Natalie also said interviewees stand out by being able to recount past achievements and speaking of them with pride. Likewise, interviewees must be real and confidently speak of times in the past when they've made a mistake. Sharing these real experiences allows the interviewer to get to know the *real* candidate, Natalie says.

It's natural to be nervous when you interview. Remember: the outcome of the interview doesn't reflect on your worth as a person. Whether you get the job or don't, try not to take it personally. In our conversation, Lou advised to practice being nervous ahead of your actual interview. When in the *real* interview your heart speeds up and you start talking fast, your practice kicks into gear. You'll be able to take a breath and regain your center.

Remember: If you fake who you are in an interview and then get hired…you've got to continue being that fake person. In interviews, authenticity wins. (*Professional* authenticity.) You're interviewing the company just as much as they're interviewing you. Be sure you like what you're signing up for.

5. Once you get the job:

You're offered a job—yahoo! Now what?

Natalie Fisher advised job applicants to express genuine enthusiasm over a job offer—yet not to commit immediately. You need time to review the job offer. In some cases, you may be able to negotiate for a better salary or different benefits. This is especially true if it's your second or third job and you've already proven yourself in the workforce.

Hopefully, you and the employer are already aligned on salary expectations once you get the offer. Perhaps the range was posted on the application; if not, it should have come up during the interview process. For a first job, here's my advice: if you've determined what you *must* make to meet your needs, and an employer offers you a job that meets that number, say yes.

Lou Adler advises candidates that "compensation is not forever, it's just for a year." Lou advises employees to look for opportunities to grow and take on more responsibility. Once you've successfully done this, you'll feel more confident asking for a raise or promotion—or if none is forthcoming, taking your skills someplace they'll be more highly valued.

6. Do your best on the job.

According to Natalie Fisher, there's a golden question you can ask in job interviews that will set you apart in the hiring process and put you on the right track once you get the job: "How can I exceed expectations in this role within the first three months?"

It's such a smart question. If you ask the interviewer this, they'll know you're serious about the standards to which you hold yourself and your work. Even better, you'll be given the criteria you need to knock your boss's socks off once you get in the role. Take notes in the interview and keep them handy. Be ready to hit the ground running from day one.

Take nothing for granted once you get in your role. Do your best, always—and document your work. Be able to show your manager *how* you've done your best—with processes, statistics, reviews, and such—so you can clearly demonstrate and articulate your value to the employer. Assume that your employer is distracted and does not always see the good work you put in. You don't have to go around bragging about it, but you do need to document. Be prepared to make the case for a raise or promotion when it's appropriate to ask for one.

Some more "Hey, Dad" advice from yours truly: Remote work is great. It's opened the labor market so you're no longer limited by your geography in what roles you can accept. However, there's a real risk (in my opinion) of being totally remote. The risk is two-pronged: First, you run the risk of not being visible to your boss. "Out of sight, out of mind"—if your boss doesn't see you and the good work you're doing, you're less likely to be promoted. Your career and earnings potential can stagnate.

Second, there's the social factor risk. Put simply: you need friends. (Everyone does.) In high school and college, you didn't have to work hard to make friends—they were just there. What happens when you get a remote role and never have a reason to leave your apartment? That situation gets depressing fast...even if it's a really nice apartment.

Remote work isn't going anywhere, and I don't want it to. I'm just saying that being a young adult isn't easy, and people make it easier. Go out and find your people. Work is a great place to do that. If your workplace offers a hybrid situation where you work part-time from the office and part-time remote, be sure you put in face time at the office: both for the good of your career and your own personal good.

One last thing: Stay out of office drama and gossip. I know it's tempting to get in the dirt. Workplace drama can feel spicy and fun and liven up work when it feels routine. But you're much better off getting your kicks elsewhere. If you're engaging in workplace drama, your work suffers...and if you think your boss doesn't notice, you're wrong. (I'm an employer. I notice.)

"Stay out of workplace drama" is also true if you're remote. Once, I was running a company-wide Zoom call. One employee sent a "private" message bad-mouthing another employee—except it wasn't private. The whole office saw, right there in the chat. I had to stop the call right there, kick all the other employees out of the Zoom, and warn the message sender. It wasn't pretty. That person learned a lesson and has never made that mistake again.

On the job, keep things positive. Remember that no workplace is perfect. Work isn't Disneyland, and it's not supposed to be. Work is sometimes boring, sometimes frustrating, sometimes less than fulfilling. Believe it or not, that's okay. Focus on doing your best and on connecting meaningfully with your peers and your leaders. Work isn't supposed to be everything in your life, so don't expect it to be. Make time for hobbies, sports, friends, more learning—whatever is meaningful to you. At the end of the day, remember that you're a lot more than your job or your paycheck. Stay in touch with what makes you *you*...on the job and off.

THE "HEY, DAD" PARTING SHOTS

Remember that where you start isn't where you'll finish. The first job you get out of college won't be the job you have for the rest of your life. The important thing is just to *start*. It doesn't matter where you went to college or what degree you did or did not get; the longer you're in the workforce, the less those things matter. What matters is your ability to get the job done—and whether or not you like it. You can't know whether you'll love or hate a particular career path until you're in it, so jump in.

People will make all the difference in your career journey, both when you're job searching and when you're employed. Good relationships with your co-workers and your boss make work fun and satisfying. While you don't have control over your boss, you do have control over the effort you put into your relationships. Reach out. Be helpful. Say "thank you" to those who give you a boost at every stage in your career journey. You never know who is noticing and what opportunities simply being a good person will lead to in the future.

Do your best on the job, but don't let your identity get wrapped up in what you do. Do the confidence-building work of showing up each day and doing the work in front of you to the best of your ability. Show yourself that you're someone you can trust. You don't want to let your boss down…but you *really* don't want to let yourself down. Make yourself proud.

TL;DR

Here are the "too long, didn't read" bullet points for everything we covered in this chapter:

- Use job websites and university placement offices to help you find a role.
- Network, network, network.
- Prepare for the interview—know the company and prepare stories to demonstrate your ability.
- First impressions are key. Show up early, be presentable, have a firm handshake, and look the interviewer in the eye.
- Answer questions in under one to three minutes. Remember, SAFW (say a few words).
- Remember this golden interview question: "What would it take to exceed expectations in this role in the first three months?" Write down the answer.

- Remember that the compensation you're offered is not forever, it's just for a year. Look for opportunities to take on more responsibilities.
- Stay out of workplace drama and gossip.
- Putting in face time at the office is a good idea, both for your career potential and your mental health.

SCRIPTS FOR NETWORKING

With someone you know (college professor, former employer, etc.):

> "Hi _____, hope you're well. How was your trip to Italy? [*Make a personal connection.*] As you probably know, I'm graduating soon and looking to start my career in _____ _____. Can you think of anyone I should have a conversation with, and would you be willing to connect us?"

With someone in a role at your dream company:

> "Hello _____, I see that you work at _____. I've admired that company for a while because of [*say why you admire it*]. I'm interested in learning more about the company; as I start my career, I believe my experience in _____ could be a good fit for the company's needs. Would you be able to talk for twenty minutes to tell me about your experience there?"

With someone who can hire you:

> "Hello _____, my name is _____
> _____. I'm a recent college graduate and excited
> about beginning my career in _____.
> I see that we both know _____ [*if you
> have a personal connection to the hiring manager,
> be sure you say so*].
>
> I really enjoyed my internship in _____
> last summer and was proud of how I [*point
> to an accomplishment you're proud of, either in
> school or in a workplace environment*]. I'd love
> to know more about your company and what
> your biggest needs are. Would you be willing to
> meet with me for twenty minutes?"

With someone in a field you're interested in pursuing:

> "Hello _____, I see that you're in
> [*your intended field*]. I am about to graduate
> with my degree in _____ and I'd love
> to know more about what the actual job is like.
> Would you be able to meet with me for twenty
> minutes so I can learn what advice you have to
> offer?"

CHAPTER 3

START A BUSINESS

How to make your own rules for work

Early in my career I lived my "dream"—working on Wall Street. And then I chucked it to do something crazy: start a business.

I started my first business when I was twenty-nine years old. I had a wife, two kids, and another on the way. Making the business successful, earning enough to feed my family, hiring employees and keeping them on payroll—it was *all* on me. With each passing day after quitting Wall Street, the weight grew a little heavier. I had to come up with cash—and *fast*.

I got a second mortgage. I sold a car, financed another so my family could have a vehicle, and put the money back into the business. I borrowed money from my 401(k) and my kids' college funds. I worked part-time jobs, in addition to spending every waking moment working to get the business off the ground.

That first year was brutal. The need for cash stared me in the face everywhere I looked. I needed legal advice to properly set up the business, which required cash. I got on every plane and went to every conference I could (cash); I passed out business cards to prospective clients (cash); I made expensive phone calls pitching our services to would-be buyers (cash); I hired people (cash). I felt tremendous pressure to make good on the loan I'd taken from my family's future—the one I'd financed myself with my retirement savings and kids' college funds. I took no money from outside investors. I had everything on the line.

Yet even amid the sleepless nights and wondering where the mortgage payment would come from that month, I felt exhilarated. I came from a family of entrepreneurs. Building a business was in my blood. In March of 2000, my business did its first sale—and the high was better than anything I'd experienced other than the birth of my children. It was the entrepreneur's drug; once I got a hit, I knew I could never go back to being someone's employee.

My kids, for better or worse, have never seen me have a boss. I've never had any of the gripes that go along with being an employee: having a manager I don't jive with, a long commute, compensation tied to how someone else views my performance, et cetera. I, my father, and my brother are all business owners; this is the model my kids have for earning a living. The one job they know is "boss." My kids have had the privilege (or misfortune) of working in my business as interns. During her internship, one of my daughters presented me with an organization chart she created; she and her dog were at the top, with me reporting to her. (She wasn't far off.) Being a business owner has been a wild ride: at turns humbling, gratifying, exhilarating, demoralizing, satisfying...and all things in between. Choosing to start a business has made for a great life for my family and me—but it's not for everyone.

If you're crazy enough to want to start a business, I won't try to talk you out of it. (I couldn't if I tried.) Entrepreneurship is not for the faint of the heart, or the super smart. Plenty of folks who made below-average grades in school find success as entrepreneurs. Book smarts aren't necessary, yet street smarts are everything. Entrepreneurs are people who see opportunities other people don't. They take risks that deter most. The best entrepreneurs have something on the line: they are personally invested in the success or failure of their business.

Do you have that level of dedication? Or are you a "wantrapreneur?" Plenty of people say they want the entrepreneur's lifestyle: freedom. Flexibility. Control over their schedules. They're not thinking about coming up with insurance for their kids or paying tuition costs for daycare. Freedom and flexibility are great—until you can't pay your bills.

I didn't have a choice: If my business wasn't successful, my family wouldn't eat. I had to do everything I could to make my business work; either that or get another job.

It's amazing what you can do when your back is to the wall.

Are you thinking of starting your own business? Here's what I'd tell my twenty-nine-year-old self, if I had to do it all over again:

1. Take an inventory of the skills you've already acquired. One of them could lead to your breakthrough business venture.

Working on Wall Street, I learned about securitization. That means taking an asset like a loan and turning it into securities, which can be marketed and sold. One day I got a call from an old client who wanted help with a securitization-related problem. That phone call planted the seed that would become my first business.

When I got my first job, I didn't know how one thing would lead to the next. Neither can you. The most you can do at any given time is your best: where you are, using what you have, with the people around you. Even if right now you're working a job that bores you to tears, don't write off your experience because you're not where you want to be. Pay attention. Right under your nose could be the seed of your future business empire.

2. Celebrate the little wins.

"Whoa—this is a real business."

That's how I felt when I hired my first employee. Having someone else on payroll means everything suddenly gets very real. I was already pouring everything I had into the business— so in theory, I knew it was "real." But hiring that first employee was like drawing a line in the sand. There was no going back.

Even though the moment was fraught with a new level of uncertainty, it was worthy of celebration. As an entrepreneur, you don't go from starting the business to making your first million (or even your first hundred) in a week. The pathway twists and turns, the destination often unclear, the goalposts shifting. That's why it's so important to celebrate the small wins you experience on the way to your goal. First client? Celebrate (even if it's your mom's friend who's known you since you were in diapers). Hiring someone to do your books? Celebrate. First employee? Celebrate. The celebrations don't have to be huge (definitely don't spend money you don't have), but mark the milestones as you pass them. Entrepreneurship is about the journey, not the destination. If you don't learn to enjoy the ride, there's no point.

3. Have something on the line.

My company now invests in other small businesses. If I'm going to greenlight a business investment, the founder must have something on the line. Unless the founder has put a significant amount of their own money into the business, I'll pass.

If you don't have something on the line, you'll give up too quickly. If you're interested in starting the type of business that requires outside investment, investors will want to see that you have a stake in the business succeeding. Why should an outside investor take a risk if you won't? If your ability to feed yourself and have a place to live hinges on your business's success, you won't throw in the towel when the going inevitably gets rough. With great risk comes great reward…if you're willing to tough it out.

4. Ideas are a dime a dozen. You can have the "perfect" idea— but does it solve a pain?

I spoke with seasoned small-business expert Barry Moltz about what it takes to make it in business. Barry is a serial entrepreneur; for the last twenty-plus years he's started many businesses, made them profitable, and then sold them. Barry now helps other business owners grow and sell their businesses. He is also the author of several books, including *You Need To Be a Little Crazy: The Truth About Starting and Growing Your Own Business* (the title says it all). Barry says that if you're going to be successful, your product or service must solve a particular pain.

People buy when they're in pain. Customers are shown a product or service that will alleviate their pain—if the promise of the product or service is great enough, customers will part with their dollars. Barry asks entrepreneurs: "What's the pain you solve? What are your customers doing right now to solve that pain? Do they have the money you're asking them to spend to solve their pain?" Entrepreneurs who can answer those questions are on their way; if they can't, they need to spend more time with the questions before they bring a product to market. Your idea isn't worth much unless it's solving your customers' pain—and they'll pay for it.

5. Starting a business is really, really hard.

I won't mince words; starting a business is extremely hard. I see it all the time; people start a business because they want to be their own boss and have more free time...and end up working more than they've ever worked in their lives. As Barry's book title says, "you have to be a little crazy" to pursue entrepreneurship rather than getting a job.

Between 95 and 98 percent of first businesses don't work out. In our conversation, Barry said that "overnight success" usually takes ten years to achieve—and it's reserved for those who have tried and failed many times. In entrepreneurship, stuff happens. Barry once tried to sell a business for ten million. Overnight, the business lost its biggest customer which had accounted for over half of its revenue. He eventually sold the business—for one million. That's life. Stuff happens; timing doesn't always work out.

You won't be Mark Zuckerberg or Elon Musk out of the gate...and probably not ever. That doesn't mean you shouldn't pursue business ownership. It means you should try something, fail, iterate, and try again until you make it.

6. Success is for the resilient.

Business ownership will teach you resilience. If it doesn't, go and do something else. The only way to succeed is to be resilient and adapt to changing trends. If you stay down when you get knocked out, your business won't make it.

Barry shared his experience: His life was on a certain trajectory before he started in business. He worked at IBM for ten years and got promoted every year—until he got fired. Barry then started his first business with a friend—and then they went out of business. He started a second business with two people he found via the newspaper classified ads…and then those two kicked Barry out. Suddenly, life wasn't so steady or predictable. Yet those times taught Barry how to keep going.

If you're crazy enough to start a business, no one will be able to talk you out of it. Yet nothing can truly prepare you for the ride that is entrepreneurship—not even entrepreneurship classes in college. What will you do when you've maxed out all your credit cards and you suddenly lose your best customer and can't make the minimum payments? What will you do when your best employee quits? When a competitor sues you to try to knock you out?

You hang in there. Sometimes you call it quits—but then you come back wiser and stronger. Success is the combination of many factors, including having a great team and hitting the marketplace at the right time with the right product. Yet you won't have those things out of the gate: you'll gain them by trying, failing, and then picking up and trying again.

7. Be humble and take care of yourself.

"I want to be an entrepreneur because I want more free time and to be my own boss."

But becoming an entrepreneur means you suddenly have a *lot* of bosses. Your clients are your boss. Your vendors are your boss. If you take outside investment, those investors are your boss. If you start a business believing people owe you something, you're already failing. No one owes you anything—and the stress of business ownership is often more than "wantrapreneurs" bargain for.

Barry said that in the '90s, he dealt with serious anxiety and depression and got type two diabetes—all from the stress of running his businesses. He didn't yet know how to moderate his life and develop his outside interests. Business was Barry's entire life—and if things weren't doing well, neither was he. That's a far cry from the image of entrepreneurship sold to us! "Wantrapreneurs" picture themselves ocean-side with a pina colada in hand as the money piles up. If someone was selling entrepreneurship with a picture of diabetes medication, no one would buy it.

Rather than strive for "work/life" balance, Barry recommends entrepreneurs aim for "integration." To Barry, this means developing identities outside of business. Barry is not just a business owner; he's a husband, father, cyclist, hiker, tech enthusiast—the list goes on. If we put our identities too much into one area, we're in trouble; what happens when that area starts to get shaky? An integrated life is a healthier, more sustainable, and more interesting life. Nothing about business ownership is short-term. It's all a long game; business owners can't burn themselves out and treat everything like an emergency if they want real staying power.

8. Find a mentor (or several).

Barry said one of the single best things you can do as a business owner is to find a mentor. One of Barry's early mentors was an entrepreneur who bought consumer toys to market. Even though their businesses were unrelated, Barry's mentor understood entrepreneurship and the startup world. He was able to ask Barry the right questions to help him consider his business in a new light.

You can't put out a fire from inside the house. That means as a business owner, you're too close to your own problems—too focused on the day-to-day grind of running your own business to see the big picture and consider where you'd like to go. So how do you find people to bounce ideas off of?

You can start by offering to take business owners you admire out to lunch and ask them for their insights. You'll probably find, as I did in my job hunt, that people are generous with their time and expertise. You can also set up an advisory board, as Barry recommends. He suggests gathering three to four people you admire and flying them to your city once a quarter. Pay them a daily rate and ask them to give you their reflections and ask probing questions, all with the intent of helping you understand your business better. According to Barry, your mentors shouldn't have a stake in your success (as in, not your employees). They should also be entrepreneurs or former entrepreneurs—people who get it. (Only do this if you can afford it! Again—don't spend money you don't have.)

The hallmark of a good mentor is someone willing to tell you the truth. As you ascend higher and higher in the business world and achieve more success, folks who will speak "truth to power" are harder to come by. Find people with enough backbone to shoot straight with you.

If you can't afford to pay mentors just yet, Barry recommended participating in business incubators and mentorship programs in your area. These are often free. Check out Y Combinator ("YC"), which is a startup accelerator that has helped launch businesses such as Stripe, DoorDash, Instacart, and Airbnb. Be aware: it's *really* tough to get into YC. In 2023, more than forty-four thousand businesses applied, and YC accepted less than 1 percent. However, most cities have some kind of business incubator program. SCORE is another good (free) resource: it's a mentoring program in which any entrepreneur or aspiring entrepreneur can request a mentor and be matched with a more seasoned business owner. (Did I mention it's free?)

Don't let "But I don't have a mentor" be an excuse standing between you and your dreams of starting a business. Start by doing the work.

9. Learn entrepreneurship on someone else's dime.

Are you intrigued by entrepreneurship but not ready to take the leap right away? That's okay—you can learn on someone else's dime. Go work for a startup.

After Barry left IBM, he went to work for someone who had been one of IBM's clients. As an IBM employee, Barry had been intrigued by this client with a thriving business. Working for this client taught Barry entrepreneurship.

Learning on someone else's dime is a great way to learn the ropes. Getting a behind-the-scenes look at a startup is an invaluable business education—more worthwhile than any college degree in business. You'll learn as much (probably more) from the startup's failures as from its successes.

When I started my business, I had everything on the line—a mortgage and a family to support. It was sink or swim. Business with a capital *B*.

But what about starting a "side hustle?" "Side hustles" weren't really a thing when I started out. But today, 45 percent of Americans have a side hustle.[2] *Self* magazine reports that most Americans work between five and ten hours a week on their side hustles, whether to create a financial cushion or cover their basic expenses.

As an employer, I admit I'm skeptical of side hustles. I want my employees to give me their best and fulfill their contractual obligations. But as a dad...I think it makes sense to have an extra income source. If working your side hustle is not detracting from your nine-to-five job, why not devote your extra hours to something that will help you generate financial stability?

"Side hustles" are not part of my lexicon, so I was curious: At what point does a side hustle tip into a full-fledged business? Jayson Siu started a side hustle that now brings in over $500,000 a year: a legitimate business by any measure. Here's Jayson's advice for side hustlers and business owners:

---

2 "Side hustle statistics: Everything to know about side hustles," Self, https://www.self.inc/info/side-hustle-statistics/#:~:text=45%25%20 of%20working%20Americans%20currently,per%20week%20 on%20their%20business.

SIDEBAR
HOW TO START A SIDE HUSTLE

Jayson found entrepreneurial success customizing car accessories with LED lights and then selling them on the internet, which he does through his company, Invalid.jp. He also runs other e-commerce stores that sell materials like women's beauty products and hydrogen water bottles. Most impressive of all? Jayson is still a student. As of this writing Jayson is a student at the University of Hawaii Manoa.

If you want to get started with a side hustle—whether you want that hustle to eventually become your business or you're looking to make additional income on top of your nine-to-five—here are three things to keep in mind:

1. **Manage your time well.**

    Jayson's shops average twenty to thirty thousand customers a month. That's a *lot* of business to keep up with. Jayson admitted it's very hard to manage the demands of his businesses with his schoolwork. He sets aside time for his significant other and has put boundaries around time pockets with family so that business will not intrude. Still—as a college student, Jayson still has to play by his professors' rules and keep up grade-wise if he wants to pass.

Managing a job, a side hustle, and a personal life will be difficult. At this stage in your life, do you have the hours to commit to a side hustle? Be honest with yourself. If the answer is no yet the desire to start the side hustle persists, consider what you could change. Are you in a busy season at work that will lighten up in a month or two? Are you spending a few months at your parents' house after you graduate, thus freeing up extra cash? Look for your opportunity and plan to make the most of it. Don't overwhelm yourself. Remember Barry Moltz and his acquired type two diabetes. No business or side hustle is worth your health.

2. **You don't need much to get started.**

Jayson estimates that he started his LED-light car accessory business for around $100–$200. His costs included a website and samples of the product he would later sell—that's it. Jayson utilized a social media page (free) to advertise his website and marketed the products by posting daily videos online (also free). According to Jayson, you don't need a lot to get started.

Jayson said he sees many would-be business owners stop because they get overwhelmed with all the things they think they need. For instance, people think they need a formal LLC. However, starting an LLC is relatively easy— and not something you need to do right away,

Jayson says. He mentioned that you can always find people to help you with the legal and financial aspects of your business as you gain success; don't let *not* having those things keep you from starting.

If you want to start a side hustle, don't overthink it. Try setting a timer for ten minutes and see how many ideas come to mind. Then, try the one that seems most doable. Successful business owners and side hustlers don't give in to "analysis paralysis"—when they have a good idea, they *move*. Try out your ideas and see what people will pay for. Once people pay you, *boom*—you've got a side hustle.

3. **A side hustle could lead to a full-time business.**

When CNBC profiled Jayson for their "Six-Figure Side Hustle" series, he had pocketed about $400,000 from his side hustle.[3] By the time this book comes out, that number may be well over $1,000,000. When you're doing business like that...why get a job?

Jayson doesn't plan to. He said he plans to do e-commerce for as long as he can. A side hustle can turn into a full-time business—and the barrier to entry is a lot lower than it was for

---

3   Megan Sauer, "21-year-old ran his side hustle from his parents' apartment—now it brings in over $500,000 a year," CNBC, October 31, 2023, https://www.cnbc.com/2023/10/31/how-college-student-built-lucrative-side-hustle-from-parents-apartment.html.

me, with my family's well-being and our mortgage on the line. According to Jayson, anyone can have a good month where they make five figures. Yet how well does the business do over six months? Twelve?

Jayson advised seeing if you can maintain consistency before going all in on your side hustle, whether you're still a student or have a full-time job. He admitted that running his side hustle is hard and not for everyone. The market is super competitive. Despite Jayson's success at such a young age, he's put in years of work—and lots of money—into making his e-commerce stores successful. Are you willing to do that? Or do you want a side hustle that's more of a monetized hobby?

For example, maybe you enjoy graphic design and want to exercise your talents outside of work. You could put up a website, a few sample portfolio pieces, and email all your friends and family to let them know what you're doing. Maybe you make a few hundred bucks, which you then sock away in a savings account dedicated to that Bali vacation on your vision board.

There's Jayson's version of a side hustle and the graphic design version…and a whole host of things in between. No one is better than the other. If you want a side hustle, just start.

Figure out your goals as you go. Pause, experiment, and reassess often.

And remember: Take care of yourself. Enjoy being a young person. You can always make money—you won't always have the freedoms and opportunities available at this stage of life. Whether you get a job, start a business, develop a side hustle that earns you an extra $100 a month or an extra $10,000…enjoy the ride.

THE "HEY, DAD" PARTING SHOTS

Some people just have entrepreneurship in their blood. I'm one of those people. You have to be a little crazy to do this, just like the title of Barry's book says. Having employees—other peoples' livelihoods—depending on *you* is something you can't prepare for. "If I screw up, my best employee might have to sell his house and take his kids out of private school"—yikes. That pressure will keep you up at night.

But the entrepreneur's high is like nothing else. Once I tasted it in the early days of my business, I knew there was no going back. Some people are just "unemployable." There's no set of characteristics that guarantees success in business. Good grades and high academic achievement aren't good predictors—in fact, there may be a negative correlation between success in school and success in business. Success in school means following the rulebook. Success in business means inventing a rulebook on the fly—and then throwing it out and starting from scratch. Over and over.

There's great risk and great reward in owning a business…
but when you get down to it, there's risk inherent in everything.
(Got a great job? Better hope you don't get fired.) Starting a
business needn't be as risky a proposition for you as it was for
me. The internet has equalized things—you have way more
access to business tools and learning than I ever did. And you
don't have to start big by quitting your job on Wall Street when
you have mouths to feed; you could start with a side hustle that
you grow over time (or don't).

Whether you intend to go big by starting a business with
a capital *B* or start small with a hobby you monetize as a side
hustle, take care of yourself. You may not have perfect work-
life balance but be sure you're nurturing your relationships
with friends and loved ones. Drink water. Eat your veggies. Get
enough sunlight. Work out a few times a week. Remember that
business ownership is a marathon, not a sprint; be sure you can
go the distance.

TL;DR

Here are the "too long, didn't read" bullet points for everything
we covered in this chapter:

- Start your business with what you know.
- Network. Nurture relationships before you need
  them for business.
- Your business should solve your customer's pain.
- Business ideas are worthless—what matters is how
  you execute those ideas.
- Take care of yourself for the long game. Spend time
  on things that bring you joy outside of business.

- Find a mentor. A great place to look is mentorship programs in your town, many of which are free (such as SCORE).
- If you're curious about entrepreneurship but not ready to take the plunge yourself, go work for a startup or start a side hustle.
- Business ownership—no matter the size of your business—requires commitment, resilience, and adaptability.

STARTING A SIDE HUSTLE? CHECK OUT THESE ONLINE PLATFORMS

Whether you want to start a side hustle selling products or services, it's never been easier to reach customers all over the world. Check out these platforms if you're looking for a place to showcase your goods:

- **Upwork:** If you'd like to spend your extra time selling your services, you can advertise them on Upwork. For instance, if you love reading and want to edit books for money in your spare time, you could make an Upwork profile and bid on jobs that seem interesting to you. Be aware, however, that you'll pay ten percent of your earnings to Upwork, and that jobs often go to the lowest bidder.

  Upwork is also a great place to find freelancers. Jayson Siu outsources his business's customer service to people he found on Upwork. If your business needs a website, a logo, copywriting—anything you don't feel qualified to produce or don't want to spend time learning how to do—check out Upwork. https://www.upwork.com/

- **Fiverr:** This is another platform where you can sell your freelance services. However, I'd recommend *finding* freelancers on the platform rather than *being* a freelancer on the platform. Many services sell for five dollars (hence the platform's name). Your work is worth more than a cup of coffee from Starbucks. https://www.fiverr.com/

- **LinkedIn:** On LinkedIn, anyone can create a "services" page. People looking for talent can search the Services Marketplace and submit proposals to qualified freelancers. Since LinkedIn is a social media platform, be aware that you'll need to post frequent content to attract clients to your services page (remember Jayson Siu's commitment to posting one video a day on TikTok—the same concept applies here). https://www.linkedin.com/

- **Mercari:** If you've got extra stuff lying around, consider selling it on Mercari. Mercari is an online marketplace where people sell secondhand goods— everything from clothing to lawn equipment. There are fees involved after you make a sale, and you'll have to ship everything out quickly. Study the rules of the platform before listing your first item. https://www.mercari.com/

- **Etsy:** Etsy is a place for makers to sell their crafts, be those paintings, custom cheese boards, or baby socks. Not all items sold are 3-D; some sellers hawk digital products such as custom spreadsheets and fillable PDFs. Etsy charges fees on top of your listing price after you make a sale, and standing out on the platform requires a visibility strategy (but that's true for all of these platforms). Experiment and see what buyers go for. https://www.etsy.com/

- **VIPKid and Skooli:** If you like working with kids, check out one of these sites. VIPKid allows you to teach English to kids all around the world. Skooli is a tutoring platform. https://www.vipkid.com/, https://www.skooli.com/

- **Airbnb:** Got an extra room? Travel frequently for work? If you enjoy traveling and hospitality, consider listing your space on Airbnb. Just be sure this is legal in your area before hosting your first guest—different cities have different laws regulating the platform. The last thing you want is a run-in with the law. https://www.airbnb.com/

- **Uber and Lyft:** If you like to drive and want to make extra cash doing it, Uber or Lyft could be a good side hustle for you. Be aware, however, that the driving will take its toll on your car. (Is the extra maintenance worth it?) https://www.uber.com/, https://www.lyft.com/

For most of these platforms, you're selling your time. Even if you make $100 an hour, there are only so many hours in a day. How could you leverage your time? What systems can you create so you're not trading dollars for hours?

Those are the questions business owners ask—and if you want to take your side hustle to the next level, those are the questions you'll be asking too.

CHAPTER 4

GET A HANDLE ON YOUR MONEY

How to be a confident money manager

Just because I *knew* about money didn't mean I was *good* with money.

That little blue book my dad had given me of financial terms when I was a kid: I knew all of them. Compounding, fiduciary, securitization—I understood what it all meant. My early career was in banking and Wall Street; for all intents and purposes, money was my life. And yet—I was broke.

In my young adulthood, if I *had* a dollar I would *spend* a dollar. I operated under the philosophy that money is no good until you spend it. I come from a family of commercial real estate entrepreneurs; entrepreneurs are, by nature, risk takers. *What's the big deal?* I thought. *If I spend money, I'll just earn it back.* I was confident—you could even say cocky. If I wasn't able to pay all my bills one month, so what? I'd be able to the next month.

The problem was, living like this soon became no fun. I got a miserable apartment that I thought I could afford—turns out I couldn't. (More on that in the "Getting a Place and Moving" section.) I didn't have money to do the things I wanted to do, simple things like go out with friends. My car payment soon became too much. I got my first "grown up" job thinking my salary of $30,000 a year would cover me for all the grown-up things I wanted to enjoy. When that turned out not to be the case, I realized I needed to reassess.

What comes to mind when you hear the word "budget"? "Boring," you may think. Or "restrictive." A "budget" version of something is the one without all the bells and whistles. Who would want to rent a *budget* car when you could rent a *luxury* car?

But just because you *can* do something doesn't mean you should. For example, if you've got real money for the first time in your life and the ability to blow $300 on a night out…should you? You may have a great time with your friends for the first hour or so; but what about afterward? Perhaps the party continues for three hours after that…three hours you're unable to recall later. You wake up the next day sometime around one in the afternoon, feeling like garbage. What did that $300 buy you? A really fun hour. What did it cost you? Three more hours you can't remember, most of the next day, and the pleasure of waking up without a pounding headache.

There are costs and benefits to everything you buy. Do you understand those? That's what a budget is all about: helping you know how much you're making, where that money is going, and if where it's going is where you *want* and *need* it to be going. Budgets are not about curbing your fun. They're about giving you guardrails so you can intentionally move in the direction you want to go. Budgets are also about helping you live within your means, so you're not stuck at the end of the month (or at the beginning of the month, or the middle) wondering where all your money went, unable to do the things you want.

Budgets are personal, because everyone has different incomes, expenses, and wants. You can never know what someone's financial situation is by looking from the outside. If you see a twenty-two-year-old on social media who is constantly taking extravagant vacations and wonder how on earth he affords them…well, maybe he doesn't. Maybe his parents are bankrolling him. Maybe that travel influencer is deep in credit card debt they'll be paying off for the next ten years. Does scrolling social media give you a sense of FOMO (fear of missing out), the desire to fork over large amounts of money on stuff you haven't really thought about? Be wary. Don't give your power away to influencers whose finances you know nothing about.

Getting a handle on your money puts you in a position of power. When you know your income and expenses and spend mindfully, you have the ability to save for things and experiences you want and set yourself up for a great future. Financial security and wealth-building don't happen all at once. They happen little by little: One debt repaid in full. One $50 moved to savings. One 401(k) opened at your job.

Think of the future you want. Blowing money might be fun for now and okay for a little while. But what kind of life do you want when you're thirty? Forty? Fifty? I bet you dream of a future where you're financially secure and able to afford all the experiences you want. Believe it or not, you're building that future *now*, with every decision you make. That's why I want you to learn good money habits while you're young. I want you to feel calm and confident—even *powerful*—about your money. That's what this section is about.

There are two chapters in this section. First, we'll look at the money that comes in and out of your life each month; chapter 4 will cover budgeting, banks, and taxes. In chapter 5, we'll look at ways to *grow* your money via the power of investments and compounding interest. Since having a good credit score is key to getting good interest rates, we'll also talk about credit scores in chapter 5. (Did that sentence make any sense to you? If not, don't worry; it will by the time you finish chapter 5.)

If the topic of money overwhelms you, that's okay. Some people get the benefit of a solid financial education from their parents; some have to learn for themselves. Regardless of where you're starting from or your feelings about money, you *can* get a handle on your finances and build a beautiful future. All you need is a little knowledge and some good habits.

HOW TO CREATE A BUDGET THAT GIVES YOU FINANCIAL FREEDOM

Today, DeShena Woodard teaches people about money management through her writing for online outlets like CNN Underscored, GoodRx, The Balance, and her life and financial freedom coaching at ExtravagantlyBroke.com. But before paying off $52,000 in two and a half years, DeShena was no stranger to financial stress. She got her first credit card at a college fair—the company's booth was set up with M&M's and balloons, designed to lure in unsuspecting young people. That was the start of the credit card trap many young people find themselves in; like many, DeShena wound up deep in credit card debt.

Her ticket out was getting smart about her finances. She learned to budget and mindfully spend; then, she and her husband became totally debt-free. Today, DeShena is a certified life coach and financial freedom coach. She teaches people to get out of debt, simplify their finances, and use their money to enjoy life. Here's what DeShena had to say about developing your personal budget:

1. A budget gives you financial freedom.

DeShena describes "financial freedom" not like some do, i.e. as the ability to stop working traditionally and live off of investments. DeShena's version of financial freedom means managing your money so that you can pay all of your expenses comfortably and still have the freedom and the options to do the things you enjoy. It's also about knowing that whatever financial goal you have, you can make a plan and eventually achieve that goal. Budgeting, says DeShena, is the key to achieving financial freedom.

Not feeling secure about money causes stress that can affect your physical health, your job performance, and your relationships. If you've lain awake at night wondering how you're going to pay rent, you know that stress. A budget is worth it for the order it brings to your finances, but also for the peace the budget brings to your mind.

2. Write your budget; don't rely on mental accounting.

Have some way of physically tracking your money; don't rely on your brain. It's too easy to underestimate your spending in certain categories and forget about others altogether. DeShena said this process does not have to be fancy; she writes her budget by hand. Whether you rely on spreadsheets, a notebook, or an app that you update throughout the week/month doesn't matter; just get a tracking system in place.

To create your budget, start with your guaranteed income. How much money do you know you'll bring in each month? Start with your guaranteed, after-tax money. If you receive a bonus, you can determine what to do with it, but the bonus shouldn't be a part of your regular budget. Then, minus your expenses from your income. To do this, go back through bank credit-card statements and look at every single thing you spent money on. DeShena recommends going back three months.

DeShena has recommended spending allotments based on needs. Keep in mind, everyone's budget will look different, because everyone has different expenses, goals, and liabilities. Here is a sample budget with that in mind:

- After-tax, take-home monthly pay: $4,500
  - Housing: 30 percent of income, or $1,350
  - Transportation (car payment, gas, auto insurance): 15 percent of income, or $675
  - Insurance (health): 5 percent of income, or $225
  - Debt repayment (such as student loans): 15 percent of income, or $675
  - Food (groceries, eating out): 10 percent of income, or $450
  - Utilities (internet, water, electric): 5 percent of income, or $225
  - Giving (to charitable causes or a spiritual institution): 5 percent of income, or $225
  - Saving: 5 percent of income, or $225
  - Fun money: 5 percent of income, or $225

If you've done the math, you'll see that budget adds up to 95 percent of a person's income. The other 5 percent serves as a buffer, in case spending is a little higher in one area each month. However, once the buffer is in your account, you won't need to include the entire 5 percent in your expenses every month. You'll only need to replace any amount that was spent.

Note that your budget *will* look different than this one; this is just a sample. Perhaps you have a paid-off car, or your office pays for you to use public transportation; your "transportation" category may be next to nothing. Or, you may live in a very expensive area and have to spend 50 percent of your take-home pay on rent. Maybe you're fortunate enough not to have any student loans to repay. You could have a goal that will require you to be aggressive with savings (for example, you want to buy a house in the next two years); thus, you decide to put 20 percent of your take-home pay into savings.

Personal finance is personal. Get clear on *your* needs and what's important to you. DeShena does offer one directive for everyone, however, regardless of income or liabilities: spend 5 percent of your money each month on fun things, just for you. You need space to enjoy your money. Otherwise, budgeting will feel too difficult and you'll resent your budget. The constraint of a budget is meant to bring freedom—not to leave you feeling trapped and joyless.

3. Pay off your debt as quickly as possible.

The faster you pay off your debt, the less you'll pay in interest. Paying off debt is especially important for debt that carries high interest rates, like credit cards.

Here's what that means; the average credit card interest rate is 21.47 percent.[4] Let's say you have a credit card debt of $5,000 and you want to pay it off in three years. Your monthly payment will be $190; over three years, you'll pay off the original debt of $5,000, *plus* an additional $1825.03 in interest. Now you've paid nearly $7,000 instead of $5,000.

DeShena recommends always paying more than the minimum required payment on debt. She also recommends everyone having an emergency fund of $1,000; that way when unexpected expenses pop up, you won't have to go further into debt to take care of them. You can save and pay off debt at the same time; once you've reached $1,000 in your emergency fund, DeShena recommends putting more toward debt.

If you're curious about the true cost of your debt and want to create a plan to pay it off, check out debt repayment calculators such as the one offered by Experian at https://www.experian.com/blogs/ask.experian/creditcard-payoff-calculator.

4. Only worry about yourself.

DeShena said being financially free is not about how much money you make. As a financial coach, she has talked to people all over the income spectrum, including one man who was making a million dollars a year...and super stressed about money. This man was convinced he wouldn't have money problems, if only he could make *two* million a year instead of one million. More money will not solve your problems; creating

---

4 Sarah Li Cain, "Average Credit Card Interest Rates: Updated for 2024," SoFi Learn, March 15, 2024, https://www.sofi.com/learn/content/average-credit-card-interest-rate/#:~:text=The%20current%20average%20credit%20card,card%20you're%20applying%20for.

good money habits and having a solid plan for your money *will*. Once you know how to take care of the money you have today, you'll be in a better position to receive more money in the future—whether that money comes from a different job, an inheritance, or any other source.

To be financially free, only worry about yourself. Don't get distracted looking at someone's new car, or someone else's business-class ticket to Fiji. You don't know what it cost for them to have those things. If you only focus on your situation, you'll get rid of most of your FOMO and money stress. Be responsible with what you have and be grateful for it. When you eventually get opportunities for *more*, you'll be ready to receive it.

As you're navigating your budget and getting your finances under control, you'll develop a new relationship with your bank. Or perhaps you'll *start* a relationship with your bank. I spoke with Matt Gromada, the head of youth, family, and starter banking at JPMorgan Chase Bank, the largest bank in the US, with over eighty-two million customers and more than 4,800 branches. He offered insights into banking and what you need to know about storing your money.

1. **You need at least two bank accounts: checking and savings.**

   Think of your checking account, says Matt, as your operations account. It's where money goes in and money comes out; the money is easily accessible for the needs you have throughout the week. A savings account is where you park your money. Whether you're saving for an emergency fund, a new car, or just a rainy day, a savings account allows you to set money aside so you won't be tempted to draw from it for everyday purchases.

When choosing a bank, be sure you choose one that is FDIC insured. FDIC stands for Federal Deposit Insurance Corporation. That means if the bank fails, your money is still safe. The vast majority of bank accounts are FDIC insured, but still—double check. Also, choose a bank that is convenient to you, with many ATMs where you live. Since you'll do the majority of your banking on your phone, look for a bank with a good digital experience. For instance, your bank's app may include budgeting tools or automatically give you your credit score. Be sure you know how to access your bank info readily so you're always aware of how your accounts look and don't accidentally overdraft.

2. **Know about overdraft.**

Overdraft means you spend more money than you have in your checking account. If you purchased something for $120 and only had $100 in your checking, you may overdraw from your account. Some banks will allow you to make the purchase; they will likely also make you pay a fee. Do you want the ability to overdraw? Know your bank's system for it.

The best practice is to *not* overdraw so you're not spending money you don't have. However, if you must—let's say rent is due and it's still a few days before you get paid—know that you're doing it and *why* you're doing it. Check your accounts regularly. Also, see if there is a service fee associated with any accounts. Your savings account, for instance, may have a monthly service fee that is waived if you keep the balance at or above a certain minimum. Plan to always have that number in the account so you avoid paying money unnecessarily.

3. **Banks are different than fintech solutions.**

Fintech stands for finance + technology. Fintech players include brands like Venmo, Cash App, and PayPal; they help people pay others quickly without cash or checks. However, fintechs are not banks. You can't get your money easily in and out of them, and if you need to talk to someone on the phone, good luck. Be sure you have money readily accessible in your bank account to cover your operating expenses; if you need to transfer money from a fintech account to your bank account, it will take several days.

SIDEBAR
CREDIT UNIONS

Maybe you've heard of credit unions—you know they're like banks, but not quite the same. What's the difference?

A credit union is a cooperative, nonprofit financial institution. It is owned and democratically controlled by its members. Members pool their funds, which the credit union can then lend out to other members via loans. Credit unions are overseen by volunteer boards of directors; this is in contrast to banks, who are answerable to shareholders. Membership in credit unions is specific; not anyone can join any credit union, as they can a bank. Credit unions are established to serve people in a specific region, with a certain employer, who are alumni of a particular school or members of a faith community... membership criteria varies by credit union and whom it was established to serve.

Because they are member-run and don't have the obligation to yield high returns for shareholders, credit unions can offer members lower interest rates on loans, such as car loans or mortgages. Credit unions are also noted for offering members a high degree of service and placing an emphasis on financial education.

The downside: accessibility. Unlike the big banks you see on every corner, credit unions have far fewer offices and may be hard to reach. However, because of the low interest rates they offer on loans, it's worth establishing a relationship with a credit union. My "Hey, Dad" advice: when you need a loan, such as a car loan, begin a relationship with a credit union and secure your financing there before going to the car lot (more on buying a car in chapter 8). You'll most likely get a lower interest rate, which means you'll pay less over the life of the loan.

4. **You must prove your identity to open a bank account.**

Banks are highly regulated and work to prevent fraud. That means when you open a bank account, you'll have to supply information proving you are who you say you are. Prepare to submit your Social Security number, birth certificate, or other form of ID, along with your previous addresses, your marital status, address, and contact details. You may feel overwhelmed having to present all this, but know all of the ID-verifying is for a reason: to keep your money safe.

5. **Understand the difference between debit and credit cards.**

When you use a debit card, you're spending money from your checking or savings account. Understand that a charge on a debit card immediately reduces the balance in your checking or savings account. When you use a credit card, the money isn't coming out automatically; you're agreeing to pay that money at a later date. A Visa or MasterCard (or other brand) can be either a debit or a credit card; look at the card to know which kind you've got.

Let's say you spent $930 on your credit card during one statement period and can only pay $510 toward the bill when it's due. You'll pay interest on the remaining $420. Recall from DeShena's experience; the longer you take to pay off your credit cards, the more you'll pay in interest. The best practice is to pay your statement balance in full at the end of each month so you pay zero interest.

SIDEBAR
TAXES

Most people will pay over a million in taxes over the course of their lifetime, making taxes the largest financial transaction they'll conduct. Plus, filing a tax return is something every eligible taxpayer needs to do every year with a specific annual deadline, making it a more serious event than something that can be blown off and wait until later. What do you need to know about taxes? I spoke with Mark Steber, senior vice president and chief tax information officer of national tax-prep firm Jackson Hewitt Tax Services. Here's what Mark has to say:

1. **Claim all your deductions.**

   According to Mark, one of the biggest tax mistakes people make is not claiming all their deductions. Two major deductions are student loan interest and mortgage interest. If you are paying either of those, claiming it on your tax returns will reduce your taxable income. If you're eligible for tax credits, you get a certain amount credited to you at tax-time. For instance, the current child tax credit is $2,000, meaning most parents can receive $2,000 per child at tax time since the child is their dependent.

   Be sure to check with your parents and make sure they are not claiming you as one of their dependents on their tax return. And make sure you're claiming other appropriate deductions and credits that you're eligible for based on a variety of factors—from your income, filing status, and more. Here is a small tax secret often misunderstood: If you leave off your tax return a beneficial tax deduction or tax credit or even tax return filing election, the IRS will *not* add it back and give you more money. If you *leave off* a tax benefit—it stays off. This is not like a store retailer finding you a store credit or an airline sending you a flight credit. The IRS does not work that way.

2. **File early to prevent fraud and get your refund sooner.**

April 15 is the official Tax Day and the longer you wait to file your taxes, the higher the likelihood someone could try to commit fraud and steal your refund. In fact, not only is it best practice, but there's no penalty for filing early. You should have received all of your tax forms from employers and banking institutions by the end of January. Keep them. You then have two and a half months before the filing deadline. The earlier you file, the sooner you get your refund; Mark said February is a great time to file. Plus, the earlier you file, that means your personal information is protected from someone trying to steal it because as soon as a

Social Security number is used on a tax return for the year, it cannot be used again.

A quick note: Two tax forms you're likely to deal with are the W-2 and W-9. A W-2 is given out by *employers to employees or workers*; it records how much an employee was paid over the course of a year, as well as the amount of federal, state, and local income tax and Social Security and Medicare tax withheld. A W-9 is a form independent contractors fill out which contains their tax identification information; this way, employers have what they need to record what they paid the contractor at the end of the year. A W-9 does not have information for tax withholding; independent contractors are responsible for paying their own taxes. Which leads us to #3:

3. **You have to pay taxes on your side hustle. Know the rules.**

Mark said if you make a dollar, that dollar is taxable. If you have a side hustle that "only" makes you $500 a year, that $500 is still taxable. However, you're eligible for deductions that reduce your tax burden, so be sure to take advantage of them. The more money you make—whether via side hustle, being self-employed, or at your job—the more high-stakes taxes become, so it's a good idea to have a professional accountant helping you.

If you expect to owe $1,000 or more on your tax bill (this category often includes small-business owners and side hustlers), then you have to pay quarterly estimated taxes. Check out the IRS's guidelines[5] if you think you may be included in that group. If you are, he recommends working with a tax professional. If you're not yet doing so, it's a good idea to start. Don't wait until the end of the year to find out you have a tax bill you're unable to pay.

4. **Keep good records.**

Keeping good records of your tax history protects you on the front end and back end. On the front end, good records can get you your full deductions—for example, if you own a business or side hustle and need to deduct business expenses. On the back end, you'll need those records in the off chance that you get audited. Mark recommends keeping tax information for seven years.

If you forget to claim something on your taxes, you have three years to fix it. For instance, let's say you're paying student loans. You can deduct the interest on those student loans and reduce your tax liability. If you forget to do it one year, you can make a change on that year's tax filings for up to three years in the future by filing an amended tax return. (The bad news: the IRS also has the ability to

---

5   "Estimated Taxes," IRS, updated August 22, 2024, https://www.irs.gov/businesses/small-businesses-self-employed/estimated-taxes.

go back and make sure they've claimed all you owe. They may find within three years that you owed something you didn't pay.) Keep good records so you (hopefully) don't have any surprises. If the IRS audits you, they won't call, email or text (be wary of scammers)—they'll send a letter. The letter will have a hotline you can call with questions. It's best to consult with a tax preparer if you get such a letter. Get help.

5. **Investment accounts offer great tax savings.**

Putting money into retirement investment accounts like 401(k)s and IRAs will reduce your tax burden. Not only do you need to be doing this for future you (you want to retire someday, right?)—you'll be helping *current* you out as well. The money you put into these accounts reduces your income, which means you'll pay less in taxes. Do future you and current you a favor; open a retirement investment account. (More on these in the next chapter.)

THE "HEY, DAD" PARTING SHOTS

Maybe the people who raised you gave you a great financial education. Maybe you got a job and opened an investment account when you were a teenager and you've been building credit since high school. If that's the case, congrats for being ahead of the pack; you already know what some people have to spend years figuring out for themselves.

On the other hand, maybe you always saw your folks financially strapped. Financial insecurity may feel second nature to you because in any given month you didn't know if the lights would be turned off, whether your folks would have to sell back the car they just bought, or if there would be enough money for the extracurricular activities you wanted to do. "Not enough" may be your default programming.

The good news: it doesn't matter where you're coming from. What kind of financial future do you *want*? You can achieve it. You can get good with money and feel confident as you're pursuing your money goals. With practical know-how and mindfulness, you can live within your means, save for the things that are important to you, and even invest. Your money past does not have to be your money future. Build positive money habits *now*—and just see how far they take you.

TL;DR

Here are the "too long, didn't read" bullet points for everything we covered in this chapter:

- Being "financially free" can mean feeling peace and confidence about money.
- Have a budget and stick to it.
- Have some physical means of keeping track of your budget (and do it).
- Pay off your debt as quickly as possible, especially high-interest debt like credit cards.
- Only worry about yourself. You can't tell someone else's financial situation from the outside.

- Open a checking account for operations and a savings account as a place to park your money.
- Debit cards take the money right out of your account; with a credit card, you'll pay the money when the statement is due.
- File your taxes on time. The earlier the better.
- You have to pay taxes on your side hustle.
- Many business owners and side-hustlers have to pay quarterly estimated income taxes. Talk with a tax pro to see if this applies to you. The more you earn, the more you'll need expert guidance.

CHAPTER 5

GROW YOUR MONEY THROUGH INVESTING

How to create a solid financial future

When it comes to money, risk is not a bad thing. You just have to make sure it's the right type of risk.

When I was in my mid-twenties, I took on a bad risk: I bought an old house. I was a young dad. I wanted to buy a house because it seemed like the natural next step for my growing family. I'd buy the house for cheap (you could do that back then) and then renovate it; in the process I'd create wealth for my family and have an asset I could pass down to my kids, eventually. I had grown up working in my dad's real estate business and doing some construction. I thought the home renovation would be easy for me.

Nothing could have been further from the truth. I soon discovered the $35,000 I'd budgeted for renovations wasn't nearly enough: I needed nearly three times that, plus the money that I'd already put down to buy the place. We couldn't live in the house while it was being renovated; we lived in a townhouse as

I paid for both places. I never got to enjoy the renovated house; we moved to New York City the following year. So much for my dream of having an asset for wealth-building.

If I hadn't been in such a rush to buy the house, I would have asked myself some questions: namely, *why?* Why did I want the house? I would have discovered that I didn't really *want* the house; I just thought I needed it. People all around me were buying houses. As a husband and father, it seemed like the responsible thing to do—a surefire way to improve my family's financial situation, the American dream. I didn't understand the nature of the risk I was taking on. And then I found myself in the terrible position of having no money, saddled with a falling-down house our family couldn't even enjoy.

I bought the house because I wanted to invest in an asset that would appreciate over time. I didn't fully understand the risk and ended up taking a major loss. Yet in terms of investments, *risk* is a good thing. With great risk comes great reward; if an investment is risky, it has the potential to drastically increase. But it can also drastically *decrease.*

I want to help you mitigate that risk. This chapter is about how to grow your money through investing. In the last chapter, we talked about the importance of budgeting and parking your money in safe places like a checking account for operational expenses and a savings account for longer-term goals. But how do you *grow* your money? Very few people "save" their way to wealth. Most people who attain wealth do so by investing in appreciable assets—that means things that become more valuable over time—such as: real estate, the stock market, or businesses.

If you don't want to have a job until you die and would like to one day retire, you need to be investing, also. This doesn't have to be intimidating. What picture comes to mind when you think of investing? You may imagine someone checking their phone every five minutes, looking to see if their stocks have gone up or down, frantically buying and selling to get in on the latest craze or ditch a stock that's underperforming. That's all very dramatic—and not at all necessary. Trust me; investing is for you, even if the concept intimidates you.

Right now, you have a huge investment advantage: time. Let's say you're twenty-two and expect to work for about forty years. Even a small amount of money put in your investment account regularly can yield huge returns, due to the magic of something called compound interest (which we'll talk about in a moment). Let's say you have a 401(k) with your employer that yields a return rate of 7 percent each year. If you put $200 a month into your 401(k) beginning at age twenty-two and retire at age sixty-seven, that investment will have grown to $758,518. Someone who started investing for retirement at age forty-two, by contrast, would have to put in $936 a month to have that same-sized nest egg. And if at age twenty-two you'd put the $200/month into a savings account rather than investing it in the stock market, you'd only have $108,000 after forty-five years! That's $650,518 you'd miss out on because you didn't invest.

I want you to build the habit of investing *now*, even if you can only afford to do that with a small amount each month. Investing is a must-do if you want to build wealth. To understand more about how this works, let's first take a look at interest, a.k.a. the "cost of money."

HOW INTEREST WORKS

There is "good" interest and there's "bad" interest. *Good* interest is the extra money *you* earn in a savings or investment account; it is your money making money. *Bad* interest is the type you have to *pay* because you've borrowed someone else's money. If you have student loans, that's borrowing someone else's money; same with credit cards. When you repay the loan, you're not just paying for the amount you borrowed; you're paying for that amount *plus* interest.

The lower the risk in a situation, the lower the interest rate. For instance, if you park your money in a major bank, it will earn a lower interest rate than if you invested it in the business of a friend who promised you a ten percent return on your investment. However, you're much more likely to get your money back from the bank.

(Pro tip: A high-yield savings account, or HYSA, is a great, low-risk place where money can grow just by sitting there. As of this writing, the average APY, or annual percentage yield, of a savings account is 0.45 percent.[6] However, a high-yield savings account may have an APY of 4.5 percent or better. That means if you had $100 in an average, 0.45 percent APY savings account, at the end of the year you would earn $0.45 in interest. If

---

6 Matthew Goldberg, "What is the average interest rate for savings accounts?" Yahoo! Finance, November 21, 2024, https://finance.yahoo.com/news/average-interest-rate-savings-accounts-203543195.html?guccounter=1&guce_referrer=aHR0cHM6Ly93d3cuZ29vZ2xlLmNvbS8&guce_referrer_sig=AQAAAMmjsnh4hLsEeasARJ4FHHDAJvot6IllLEARSB_cwas18kEJdseTOafK-6kaKlHj47jUW3YbKXyH7QBmPGqPYF5fiD-sA9DFM-JbqUASD9NxCCsJ1arT9sHsdTPdqkWDwCIoeXaGQM03FXo-A6UnU8tTolfQW7xjDkLhhVIAjpj7Y-a.

you had $100 in a 4.5 percent APY high-yield savings account, you'd earn $4.50 in a year...just by letting your money sit.)

A rate of return of 7 percent or more in the stock market is considered "good." For longer-term investments, a 10 percent rate of return is considered excellent. (If you hear someone talking about how they get a 20 percent rate of return with zero risk, don't believe it.) Bear in mind that the stock market will have dips, and some years your investments will not earn 10 percent. Yet the longer you're in the market, the better off you'll be. Take a long view; you don't need day-by-day analysis of what the stock market is doing if you're steadily putting money away in a retirement account that you'll open in forty years.

Here's where interest gets really exciting: compounding.

Compounding means earning interest on your interest— and it's where the real magic happens in wealth-building. When you reinvest your earnings, they start to generate their own earnings; this leads to exponential growth over time.

Consider this scenario: You invest $100 at an annual interest rate of 10 percent. After the first year, you earn $10 in interest, making your total $110. In the second year, you earn interest on $110, not just your original $100. This cycle continues; over time, your investment grows much faster than it would with only simple interest.

Here's a basic illustration of how compounding works:

1. Year 1: $100 x 10% = $10 (Total: $110)
2. Year 2: $110 x 10% = $11 (Total: $121)
3. Year 3: $121 x 10% = $12.10 (Total: $133.10)

In ten years, you've doubled your money to $259.37... without ever adding another penny to your initial $100 investment. The amount of interest earned each year increases because you're earning interest on increasingly larger amounts.

Another example: Let's say you set aside $200 a month to put in a high-yield savings account that earns 5 percent interest. At the end of ten years, rather than having $24,000 ($2,400 a year x ten years), you'd have $31,407.06! In twenty years, you'd have $82,857.26...after thirty years you'd have $167,681.41.

The "Hey, Dad" advice is to start investing early and often, and to put your money in safe places where it will have room to grow (like an FDIC-insured high-yield savings account, an employer-sponsored retirement account, a brokerage account, and other investment accounts).

I mentioned that interest can be "good" or "bad." We'll look at *bad* interest later in this chapter when we examine credit scores: what they are, why they're important, and what you can do to change yours. But now you may be thinking: Okay, I get the concept of investing. I understand that it's a good idea to put my money where it will grow. But how do I do it? Am I supposed to individually pick stocks, or does someone else do that for me? How do I open an account? Do I need a financial advisor?

To answer all those questions, I spoke to Ryan Viktorin, CFP®. She's a financial advisor with Fidelity Investments, one of the country's leading financial services companies that helps 51.5 million individuals feel confident about their most important financial goals. Ryan helps de-mystify financial jargon so her clients can understand what they're doing with their money and feel confident in their financial decisions. If you feel unsure of investing and don't know if it's for you or how to take the first step, Ryan has practical guidance for you:

1. Investing is just one part of your overall financial picture.

Investing is an important part of growing your wealth and your overall financial health—but it's just one part. Think holistically. Each month you have income and expenses. What's left over is your savings. If you want your money to grow, you can invest those savings into places where they'll potentially earn more than they would sitting in a bank account.

However, Ryan says it's critical to build up an emergency savings fund of three to six months' worth of expenses before putting more money toward investments. In other words, your savings fund *does* just need to sit in a savings account. That money needs to be easily accessible so you won't go into debt should you have a financial emergency.

2. Take a "who, what, when" approach to investing.

Ryan says you need to ask yourself three questions:

1. Who am I investing for? (The answer may be "just me"—and that's okay.)
2. What am I investing for?
3. When will I need the money?

Let's say you are twenty-two and investing for your retirement. You anticipate working for forty years. In that case, you can be more aggressive with your investing and purchase stocks that are considered "riskier" and have high growth potential (more on the process of choosing investments within a portfolio later).

On the other hand, if you want to buy a house within the next two years, your saving and investing strategy will look different than your retirement investing. For retirement, you may place your money in a 401(k); for a mortgage down payment, it may make more sense to park your money in a savings account. To choose an appropriate investing strategy, start with your goal. Know your timeline for the investment and if there are penalties for drawing out your money early.

3. Understand the different types of investment accounts.

If you have an employer-sponsored retirement account like a 401(k) and contribute to it...good news! You're an investor!

You may not think of yourself as such because a set amount of money from your paycheck goes into the account each month. Yet you are still investing in the stock market by taking this action, even if you're not actively thinking about which stocks, bonds, ETFs, index funds, and other investments make up your portfolio (more on those in a minute).

For clarity's sake, here's a rundown on the basic types of investment accounts:

1. **401(k) and 403(b):** These are employer-sponsored retirement accounts. If you work for a for-profit company, you'll have access to a 401(k); if you work for a nonprofit, it's a 403(b). The money you put into these accounts is pre-tax, so when you contribute, you're reducing your taxable income for the year. If you have an employer who matches your 401(k) or 403(b) contribution...*take advantage of it*! This is the closest thing that exists to "free

money." (Note: If you change jobs, you're able to take the money in your retirement account with you.)

2. **IRA:** This stands for "individual retirement account." You contribute your pre-tax income and reduce your tax liability.

3. **Roth IRA:** Like a traditional IRA, except you contribute after-tax income; when you withdraw at retirement, the money is not taxed. (There are income limits on who can contribute; current regulations state that individuals who make $161,000 or more cannot contribute to a Roth IRA.)

4. **HSA:** This stands for "health savings account." It's a tax-advantaged way to save for qualified health expenses.

5. **Brokerage account:** This is an individual investment account. It doesn't offer current or future tax savings. You can open an account online through platforms like Fidelity or other financial services; you either buy the investments yourself, or open an account that is managed (by a human or robo-advisor). The money in a brokerage is subject to taxes if there are gains and the value increases.

Remember that funding these accounts is a two-step process, says Ryan: first you put the cash in the account, then you purchase the investment. Sometimes you have a fund that purchases investments for you; for example, a target-date fund. This is common if you have an employer-sponsored 401(k), for example. You may say your anticipated retirement date is thirty-five years in the future. Based on that target date, your investments are diversified automatically to include a portfolio of stocks, bonds, and such. If you have longer until retirement, your portfolio will carry riskier, higher-growth potential investments; if you're closer to retirement, it will rebalance toward less-risky investments. The great thing is you don't have to think about it; you simply fund the account from an amount in your paycheck each month.

That's not the case if you open a brokerage account—which, unlike 401(k)s, 403(b)s, and HSAs, are not offered through your employer. However, it's very easy to open a brokerage account online through the financial institution of your choosing. Check to see if you're required to put in a minimum investment to keep the account open and if there are any fees associated with making purchases. If you'd like help picking investments you can turn to a robo-advisor, which is exactly what it sounds like. You can answer questions about yourself and your goals and the robo-advisor will choose your investments for you and rebalance them as necessary. This is a great option for people who want to get into the market but don't feel confident.

Pro tip: If your employer offers matching contributions for your 401(k), take advantage of it. This is as close as you'll get to earning "free money." Let's say your employer offers a dollar-for-dollar 401(k) match and you as an employee can contribute up to 5 percent of your income per year. That means if your salary is $60,000, you can contribute up to $3,000; your employer will match you and contribute an additional $3,000, bringing your total contribution to $6,000 for the year. Due to the magic of compounding interest and time in the market, that extra $3,000 can go a long way in your wealth-building journey.

4. Understand the different types of investments.

I've thrown around a lot of words like "stocks," "bonds," and "mutual funds"…but what do all of those mean? Here's a quick primer:

- **Individual stock:** If you own stock in Apple, for example, that means you own a small slice of Apple and you get a share of its assets and profits.
- **Individual bond:** A bond is a loan. If you purchase a bond, you're lending money to an organization, such as a corporation or government. In turn, you get repayment on that loan plus interest. (Bonds are typically more stable and less risky than stocks, so when you get closer to retirement, your portfolio will have more bonds in it.)
- **ETF:** An ETF stands for "exchange traded fund." It bundles together many stocks or bonds in a single investment and can be traded throughout the day.
- **Mutual fund:** A mutual fund also bundles togethers stocks, bonds, or other investments into a single fund. Mutual-fund companies, banks, and brokerages buy and sell mutual funds; unlike ETFs, they are not bought and sold between individual investors. Also, they are sold at the end of the day rather than throughout the day.
- **Index:** A hypothetical portfolio that tracks a section of the market. Two examples in the US are the Dow Jones Industrial Average and the S&P 500.
- **Index fund:** A fund whose investments track a market index, such as the S&P 500. Many index funds are structured as mutual funds.

Getting started with investing can be confusing. Work with a brokerage firm until you understand the specifics. There is no one-size-fits-all. Start with what you know—I tell my kids to pick a few stocks they understand (usually big brand names like Amazon, Nike, or Apple). Buy the stock and hold, and then put the rest of your investing dollars into a fund(s) that makes the most sense for you (whether that's an employer-sponsored 401(k), a Roth IRA, or something else). See what your stocks do. If you can't afford to buy a full share of a particular stock yet, buy a fractional share. Just get in the game, as soon as you can.

I get that it's tough to wrap your head around all these terms if they're new to you. Ryan said financial jargon can be confusing; she works hard to simplify the lingo to her clients. Fidelity has great resources online to help you wrap your head around investing and feel confident about your money plan.

5. Keep a slow and steady approach to investing.

Ryan said it's best to start investing early. Now, in your early twenties, is an *amazing* time to get into the market, which could be as simple as opening a 401(k) with your employer. Ryan said your financial priorities should be building up your emergency savings; then, you can invest with as much, or as little, as you want. You don't have to know everything, or even *close* to everything. Just get started.

Ryan said investing can be emotional, especially if you're new to it. You're putting away your hard-earned money. What happens when the market dips and you *lose* money?

Understand that these dips are natural, said Ryan. There's no need to check your account every day. You'll be in this for the long haul; take a slow and steady approach. Build the muscle of investing regularly until it feels natural. You can log into check your accounts quarterly (no more than monthly) and see if you're still tracking to your goals—if not, or if your goals have changed, you can change your strategy. There's no need to panic or go on a buying or selling spree. Think of the tortoise and the hare; slow and steady wins the race.

SIDEBAR
CREDIT SCORE

Much of our society runs on credit. You need good credit to be approved for loans for major purchases, like a car and a house. Enter the "credit score:" a number that tells lenders how likely you are to repay the loan. What actions can you take to improve your credit score? How are scores calculated? What's a "good" and a "bad" score? I spoke with Rod Griffin, senior director of public education and advocacy for Experian, to get his insights. Experian aggregates information on more than one *billion* customers, including businesses and 235 million individual users. Rod was previously named Educator of the Year by the Institute for Financial Literacy. *This guy knows credit.* Here's what Rod thinks you need to know about credit scores:

1. **A credit report and credit score are not the same thing.**

    Rod says to think of your credit report as the work you've put in for a class for the semester: your homework, test grades, papers, and such. Your score is your final grade. You can change your score by changing the things that make up the report, just as you could redo a lousy test (if your professor lets you) to get a better grade. One popular credit-scoring rubric is FICO (which stands for "Fair Isaac Corporation"), though that is not the only scoring system out there.

2. **Pay your bills on time and keep credit card balances to a minimum.**

There are two main factors that influence your credit score: your bill payment history and keeping your credit card balances low. Pay your bills on time (credit cards, car loans, or other debts); if you're a using credit card, the best practice is to pay it off, in full, each month. This will improve your credit score and keep you from paying the credit card's interest rates on the remaining balance. You might also consider enrolling in a service that lets you have your positive cell phone payments, utility bills, internet streaming services, insurance payments, and potentially your positive rent payments added to your report as well. Doing so may be helpful in building your credit history and scores as you prepare for other major purchases.

3. **Check your credit report.**

There's a common misconception that checking your credit report will hurt your credit score. This is not true. Review your credit report, especially if you're trying to build or improve your credit. Check to make sure you recognize all the purchases listed. If you suspect fraud, contact your credit card company to dispute the charge(s).

If you're planning to make a major purchase, like a car, start monitoring your credit well in advance of your intended purchase (at least three but preferably six months). You can sign up for free credit monitoring via a major credit bureau, like Experian (Rod's company) or another bureau such as TransUnion or Equifax. Making on-time monthly payments is one of the most significant ways to build credit. Beware: late payments will hurt your credit score.

Another way to build credit if you've never had a credit card; open a card and make a small purchase each month. Pay in full. Continue. This shows lenders you can easily live within your means and will pay back whatever loan they give you—in other words, that you're low risk. Just like investing, time is your friend when it comes to building credit; start early so you're in a position to make all the big financial moves you desire down the road.

4. **Know your credit score.**

What's a "good" credit score? Most people think of credit scores on a scale of 300 to 850, Rod said. However, this isn't entirely true.

There are different scores associated with different purchases; for example, a general credit score is different than the score you'd see if you wanted to get an auto loan, because the score for auto loans can go up to 900. Generally speaking, the closer you are to 850, the better off you are. A FICO score of 740–799 is considered "very good."[7]

Having a good credit score is important for two reasons. First, a credit score will allow you to make a major purchase, like a car or house. Second, a *good* credit score will get you a better interest rate. Generally speaking, the better your credit score, the better your interest. Remember good interest and bad interest? Interest that *you* pay on loans is "bad" interest. The better your credit score, the lower your interest rates—which means you keep more money in your pocket.

5. **Do not take financial advice from social media.**

Rod mentioned a scheme he saw promoted on social media which involved, essentially, committing fraud to dispute fraudulent charges. This "tactic" was promoted as a quick fix for people who have bad credit. However, there *is* no quick fix to improve your credit; good credit is a result of on-time payment history and responsible credit usage over time.

---

7   Ibid.

If someone is telling you about a scheme that seems too good to be true...it likely is.

The bottom line: good credit is very important. Many employers can (and do) check your credit report when considering hiring you, although it is important to understand they do not get credit scores and you must give the employer written permission to check your credit report. You need credit to take on car loans and mortgages; you need *good* credit to get better interest rates on those loans. Good credit means you get to keep more of your money and have access to better opportunities. You don't need to be scared of your credit report and credit score; start building credit today and do the boring actions—like paying your credit card bills on time and keeping your balances low—which will, over time, improve your credit. That's the only "scheme" there is.

THE "HEY, DAD" PARTING SHOTS

Risk doesn't have to be a bad thing. When it comes to building wealth, risk is *necessary*—but you want to make sure it's the right kind of risk. You don't have to do what I did and buy a house you can't afford, nor do you have to get in on the latest investing craze. In fact, you should do neither of those things. Investing and wealth-building shouldn't feel like a white-knuckle roller coaster ride; by contrast, it's a series of small, regular actions, repeated over time. Building wealth comes down to having good habits, as simple as socking an extra $50 a month into an investment account or paying your rent on time. You may not think these things matter—but they absolutely do. Right now, you're building a financial foundation for the rest of your life. Make it a good one—and when it comes to investing, *just do it.* The more boring, the better.

TL;DR

Here are the "too long, didn't read" bullet points for everything we covered in this chapter:

- Interest is the cost of money.
- Good interest is the money you get paid; bad interest is the interest you pay.
- Compounding is when your interest starts making interest.
- Save up a three-to-six-month emergency fund so you won't go into debt if you have to pay for an emergency.
- 403(b)s, 401(k)s, and HSAs are all employer sponsored. Take advantage of them. Other accounts you can open on your own include IRAs, Roth IRAs, and individual brokerage accounts.
- The two best things you can do to improve your credit are pay your bills on time and pay off your credit cards each month.
- You need credit to get a loan for major purchases, like a house and car.
- Don't take financial advice from social media. Just don't.

CHAPTER 6

GETTING A PLACE
AND MOVING

How to feel great about where you live

I wouldn't wish my first apartment on an enemy.

It was on Route 1 in North Brunswick, New Jersey—directly across from a strip joint and a liquor store. There was a lot of crime in the area. For recreation, the apartment had a basketball court—which I didn't dare set foot on. I picked the apartment because it was cheap—but even though I *thought* I could afford the place when I signed the six-month lease, I soon realized I really couldn't. The $650-a-month rent sometimes put me in the red. At the time, I was making thirty grand a year at Midlantic Bank. I had to pay for rent—but I hadn't counted on all the other expenses I needed to pay for as well. Water, gas, electric, groceries: all my money went to the basics, and each new bill was a shock to my newly graduated self. Who knew food was so expensive? Then there were all the little items that needed to be replaced often: paper towels, toilet paper, dish soap, and so on. All those things added up.

There was a Pathmark grocery store near my apartment where I bought the basic necessities. I ate solo meals of sandwiches and microwave dinners in my (unfurnished) living room. I had no social life, no dates—I couldn't afford them. When my six-month lease was up, I got out of that place: thus ending the loneliest, most pathetic period of my young adulthood.

As a new college graduate, I didn't know how to pick an apartment I could afford and that I'd *enjoy* living in. I didn't know the true cost of renting; that what I'd owe each month would far exceed the amount I was paying in rent. Getting the balance right between what you need and what you want in a living situation can be tricky. As I write this, the cost of living is exceptionally high. Your starting salary may not support your dream living place; but hopefully, your first apartment will check enough of your boxes so that the positives of your living situation outweigh the negatives.

What do you *need* in a home? We all have a basic need for safety, but there are a lot of other factors that contribute to our satisfaction besides the neighborhood crime score. How close is your commute to the office (if you have one)? Does your living place allow for pets? What kind of recreational amenities are offered—does the complex have a pool? A gym? Is it downtown in a walkable area, or off the freeway in a suburb? And how much do each of these things matter to you?

I hope you have a better experience than I did in my first apartment: sitting in the dark eating ramen noodles by the side of a busy road and paying too much for a crappy, unsafe place. For this section, I talked to experts on renting and moving who'll tell you what to look for in a place to live, how to understand your lease, and how to handle the (often overwhelming) task of moving. First, I spoke to Toni Eubanks. Toni is the executive director for Greystar, which is the largest apartment manager in the US. Greystar runs over three thousand rental properties, which collectively house over 1.5 million residents. As of 2023, Greystar had over $76 billion in gross assets under management and operated in seventeen countries. (It's likely *you're* living in a Greystar property!) When it comes to renting and relations between residents and landlords, Toni has seen it *all*.

Next, I spoke with Charlie Nebe. She's a YouTuber who moved seventeen times in ten years. (Yes, you read that correctly.) Both Charlie and Toni have words of wisdom for figuring out what you can afford, making sure your living situation is safe, picking a neighborhood you'll enjoy, meeting people in your new home…and everything else that goes along with building a home you want to come back to.

1. Budget at least 40 percent of your income for rent.

Toni Eubanks said that as a general rule, try not to spend more than forty percent of your income on rent. It's best if your monthly take-home pay is at least three times as much as your rent. Remember you won't just be paying rent, you'll be paying for utilities, too. Toni said renters will usually pay a fee through the rental company for trash pickup: the other utilities (internet, electric, water) renters secure and pay for on their own.

Charlie Nebe said if you *think* your budget for rent is $2,000 a month, you should be looking at $1,500/month apartments to account for the additional bills you'll need to pay. She recommends having a firm "cutoff number" and not looking at apartments outside of your budget. (This is why it's important to know your budget when you're apartment-hunting—a.k.a. the point of chapter 4.)

2. Rent from professionally managed apartment complexes.

Professionally managed rental complexes have to do things the "right" way, says Toni. They care about resident ratings for their properties. They can't cut any corners and have to keep everything in line with the law. If you rented from an individual, by contrast, that individual may not have everything up to code. There also may be ambiguous terms with the lease; for instance, you could rent from an individual and then find out you're supposed to be taking care of the lawn (or changing the air filters).

Another reason to go with professionally managed rental complexes: they usually have more amenities such as a pool, gym, dog park, or other perks. (Which amenities are important to you? Think about that before you begin your apartment search.) A professionally managed unit will also allow you to schedule apartment viewings with more ease. Charlie said during the ten years in which she moved seventeen times, if she was in a situation where she needed to find a place *fast*, she would go through a professionally managed rental community. Charlie recommended looking up the biggest rental companies in the area and going through their leasing system. You can use an apartment broker in your area to get this info or do an internet search and find a website that aggregates rental info and allows you to compare different units.

3. Tour the neighborhood in person.

When you're beginning your rental search and narrowing down your options, check out virtual maps of the area. What is the

Google Maps street view like? Is it right by a highway? Is there a building across the street with a lot of broken windows? Trash on the street? A Google Map street view check and internet search on crime in the area can weed out a lot of apartment possibilities. Toni recommends going and laying eyes on the apartment, too—especially for your first apartment. The internet can only tell you so much; your eyes and ears will tell you a lot more. Is this a place you'd feel safe and comfortable living?

Charlie said when she and her partner were moving around frequently, they'd often look for the cheapest place they could find. However, if the neighborhood was dicey, they'd find room in their budget to get a safer place. For instance, if Charlie and her husband were touring a neighborhood and saw a lot of bars on windows...then it was time to look somewhere else. Safety is most important. You want to get *out* of your apartment and meet people, not stay holed up inside all the time because you're too scared to go out. An apartment realtor can also help you out here; you can ask the realtor questions about the neighborhood(s) you're touring.

4. Read your lease carefully.

A lease is a legally binding document. When you sign, you're agreeing to abide by the financial terms set by the management company. Pay close attention. How long is the lease you're signing? When do you need to notify management to say if you're renewing the lease? Get clear on these pieces of information. Also, know that a lease is a "buyer beware" document—not something that's up for negotiation.

Consider how long of a lease you need. A twelve-month lease will generally be the most cost-effective for you; short-er-term leases will be more expensive. A professionally managed rental company will be able to accommodate any lease length you need (one month, eight months, etc.). Breaking a lease early will cost you—remember, a lease is a legally binding document. Just because you need to end a lease early doesn't mean you're not responsible for rent; Toni said a typical cancellation fee is one month's rent. If something happens with your financial situation—for instance, you lose your job—talk to your apartment manager. A professional apartment manager should direct you to available financial assistance.

5. It's okay to try out different cities.

Charlie said when she graduated college, she had a strong urge to see as much of the world as she could. Charlie grew up in Texas and lived there for the first eighteen years of her life. She watched her four older siblings get married and settle down very soon after school—Charlie knew she didn't want that. She had a visceral need to *get out* and see some stuff. Hence, moving seventeen times in ten years.

Remember Dr. Lisa Miller's advice to "go shopping" for your career? Charlie did that with places to live. She said it's normal not to know where you want to be when you first become independent. Charlie tried a lot of different things: work-away programs in Europe, working at Disney World (on their college program), working at Carnival Cruise Line, renting furnished rooms from people she knew. She didn't want to settle down until she found someplace that felt right; in some cities, Charlie lived for only a month. Charlie could do this because she didn't have a lot of possessions weighing her down. She prioritized working experiences in which her lodging would be taken care of, such as working on cruise ships. Charlie dedicated her young adulthood to having new experiences and seeing more of the world, rather than buckling down and making a lot of money.

If you want to see more of the world and experience living in different places, how could you accomplish that? Get creative. Maybe you take a job in which you'll travel frequently; maybe you work on an organic farm in another country where your lodging is taken care of. Follow your curiosity. You don't have to stay in the state where you were raised, or in a city you moved to for a job you end up hating. You get to choose where you live. That's the fun of adulthood.

6. Don't accumulate a lot of stuff.

If you see yourself moving several times before you settle down, don't acquire a lot of stuff. Consider renting furnished rooms or living in lodging provided by your employer (if that is available). Think of it this way: anything you acquire, you'll eventually have to move or sell. Moving furniture can be expensive. It's probably more cost-effective to sell furniture you acquire and start fresh in your new location—which is why you don't want a lot of stuff in the first place.

Charlie didn't rent a "regular" apartment until she was twenty-five. Before then, she lived in college dorms, on cruise ships, and in spare rooms. That was an intentional decision because she didn't want the responsibility of managing *stuff*—Charlie knew she was a long way from settling down. How much do you have weighed against how much you really need? Charlie advocates trimming down your wardrobe essentials; for a long time, she had only a few pairs of shoes because shoes take up a lot of space. She advises to not get a pet until you know you're settled. Charlie also recommends not taking up hobbies that require a lot of bulky equipment. Anything you have, you'll need to move—to your new location or into storage—or donate. Choose your possessions wisely.

7. Have a moving checklist so you don't forget anything important.

When you move into a place, you have to set up your utilities: water, electric, internet, and such. When you move *out*, you have to shut off those services. Call your utilities companies at least two weeks prior to your move-out date and let them know you'll be leaving so they can send you a final bill and shut off the services.

Each lease should have requirements regarding how to move out. If you know you'll be leaving, study your lease prior to moving so you're not caught off guard by any of the terms. For instance, cleaning: you'll most likely need to clean the apartment thoroughly before you move out. You can't just pack up your stuff and go (unless you want to pay fines for *not* cleaning). Review the standards set forth in the lease. Don't forget the little things you need to return, like your mailbox key. Have a checklist for each action item you'll need to take care of in your move, from calling the utility company to filing a new address with the post office. Charlie said that in her earlier moving days, she didn't know that canceling internet service meant you had to return the router to the service provider. She forgot to do that—and ended up having debt collectors call her for three years, chasing her for the $80 she owed to AT&T. If you're unsure how to end a service contract, just call the company and ask.

8. Be clear on your intentions for your living space.

What is your home to you? Maybe you want to live in a super expensive area, like New York City. You find the cheapest place you can, which ends up being a basement apartment the size of a walk-in closet. But you don't care; you're out enjoying the city all the time, and "home" is just a place to crash.

On the other hand, maybe you're someone who will work from home often. You need home to be comfortable—and presentable on Zoom calls. Be honest about what you need and want from a home. This will help you make decisions about where you live, how big a space to get, whether or not to live with a roommate, and so on.

9. Make an effort to meet people.

Whether you're an introvert or an extrovert, you'll be happier if you know a few people where you live. A 2022 study showed that the more you talk with different types of people in a day, the happier you'll be.[8] To maximize happiness, talk with people you have different relationships with—for example, a significant other, a sibling, colleagues, and strangers at the laundromat. Obviously, the type of conversations you'll have with each person differ; yet the study finds the greater a person's "relational diversity," the happier the person.

Get to know work colleagues. If you have an in-office component to your job, be intentional about fostering relationships with your co-workers. Enroll in a class in your new city; join a running group or a faith community. Say hello to people in line

---

8 Hanne K. Collins et al., "Relational diversity in social portfolios predicts well-being," *PNAS*, vol. 119, no. 43 (October 2022): e2120668119. https://www.pnas.org/doi/10.1073/pnas.2120668119.

at your favorite coffee shop; talk with the Trader Joe's checkout people. Each interaction will add to your happiness portfolio.

10. Have basic medicine on hand for when you get sick.

If you feel a cold coming on, what do you do? How do you stave off seasonal allergies? What's your medicine and rest routine for a headache?

When you're away from your parents—or whoever took care of you when you got sick—you'll need to stock your own personal mini-pharmacy. Vitamin C packets, pain medication, allergy meds, heat packs; think of the things you regularly use to keep yourself up and running. Stock up on your personal pharmacy when you don't need to. If you're in a new city and don't have anyone to make a CVS run for you, it's no fun to get yourself to the store when you've got a pounding headache and fever of 102.

SIDEBAR
RENTER'S INSURANCE

Renter's insurance protects you if something happens to your stuff. It also protects landlords if there's an accident at your place—for example, a kitchen fire that damages the walls. *Not* having renter's insurance isn't against the law, unlike auto insurance, which is a legal requirement for vehicle owners in most states. However, many landlords require residents to have renter's insurance in the terms of their leases.

Mark Flockhart is an insurance expert and the founder and co-owner of Valor Insurance. His YouTube channel, "Think Insurance," teaches tens of thousands of people about insurance, including how to get better coverage for less money. Mark said there's no need to freak out about renter's insurance. It's usually extremely affordable—even more so when bundled with auto insurance. You can expect renter's insurance to cost $18–$30 a month. If you need to add it to your car insurance policy, call your insurance company. Also, you want the "full replacement cost" covered in your policy. Here's what that means: Let's say you purchase a couch for $1,500. Your furniture and other possessions depreciate quickly; after a few years, the couch may be worth only $300. If something were to happen to it, an insurance company might give you $300 for it—but not if you've covered it under the "full replacement cost." Then, you get the full replacement value, which is whatever the value of the closest model to that couch is. It could be $1,800 if the value has gone up or be $900 depending on how much it is to replace that item.

If you have anything that's exceptionally valuable—let's say, an heirloom ring from your grandma—you can get a rider for that item to be covered up to its full value. That will be more expensive, though; a cheaper option is to go with a $20,000 blanket policy for everything, or $50,000—whatever you need based on your situation. Just make sure there is not a limit per item if you have a higher-value item like your grandma's heirloom ring. At this stage of life, you probably don't own things that are super valuable (especially if you're taking Charlie's advice and limiting your possessions).

However, you'll likely *have* to have renter's insurance at one point or another to abide by your landlord's lease terms. Go with the most affordable option that covers your basic needs and bundle it with car insurance when you can. Even though it would be a separate policy, it does make it cheaper if you combine auto and renter's with the same company, meaning you buy two policies, you get a multi-policy discount.

THE "HEY, DAD" PARTING SHOTS

It's okay to "shop" for a place to live, just like you can go shopping for your career. It's okay to not know where you'll end up. It's natural to want to stretch your wings and move somewhere far from home, even if that thought is scary to you. There's no rush to buy a house, get married, or do any of the things associated with settling down. You can travel with a light pack. In fact, I recommend it; you don't know how a place will suit you until you spend time living there. There's no need to commit to a place where you're miserable (I'm thinking of my six months eating ramen off the highway in New Jersey).

Whether or not you live with a roommate, on your own, go on an adventure working on an organic farm overseas, move to a bustling city or work on a cruise ship—it's all up to you, and you can change your mind when you choose. (Just be sure you read your lease carefully so you understand the cost of changing your mind too early.) Be honest about what kind of experiences you want, and what kind of housing situation will support you as you go after those experiences. Aim to strike the right balance between safety, affordability, and comfort. Explore your neighborhood; meet people, make friends. Get some numbers of people you can call if you need a helping hand and be ready to lend one in return. It's people who make a house a home.

TL;DR

Here are the "too long, didn't read" bullet points for everything we covered in this chapter:

- Budget at least forty percent of your income for rent.
- Remember that you'll have to pay for utilities and apartment fees on top of rent.
- Rent from professionally managed apartment complexes.
- Visit the apartment in person, especially when you're renting your first apartment.
- Read your lease carefully. Know that if you end the lease early, it will cost you—typically, one month's rent.
- You can "go shopping" for a place to live. If you anticipate moving around a lot, keep your possessions low.
- When it's time to move, have a checklist for all the things you need to do: cancel utilities, clean, return mail key, etc.
- Be clear on what your home will be to you: just a place to crash, or somewhere you'll be spending all your time?
- For your well-being, make an effort to meet people where you live.
- Be sure you've got basic medicine on hand for when you get sick. (Pro tip: Be sure it's not expired.)

CHAPTER 7

FURNISHING AND CARING FOR YOUR PLACE

Make your place feel like home

"Hey, Dad, how do I change my air filters?"

My daughter had a lease that required her to change the air filters in her apartment. In my opinion, that's a little much to ask of a resident. But the job is simple enough (and actually, very important).

"You just go to the metal grate on the wall and open it up. See what size is in there and replace it with the same size filter."

"I don't think so, Dad," said my daughter.

"What do you mean?" I'd changed many an air filter throughout my life—and here was my twenty-something daughter telling me I didn't know what I was talking about.

"I opened up the system and there *is* no air filter. Maybe it didn't have one. So how do I know what size to get?"

My daughter showed me what she was talking about via FaceTime—and she was right. There was no filter where one was supposed to be.

That's an instance of a landlord or past resident not doing their job. Whether this was an intentional oversight or not, the principle is the same: you the renter will need to be careful about what you agree to in a lease, especially if the landlord is asking you to take on basic maintenance. I get a lot of "Hey, Dad" calls involving maintenance. "Dad, my electricity's out. What do I do?" or, "Where's my circuit breaker?" or, "How do I stop the toilet from leaking?"

For this chapter, I spoke to Jeff Thorman, a former contractor who teaches millions of people via his YouTube channel, @ HomeRenoVisionDIY, how to care for their space—from circuit boards to air filters, and all things in between. I also spoke with Niki McNeill Brown. She's an interior designer who's been featured on the HGTV show *Design Wars*; she was also on the design team of the Emmy-winning show *Elbow Room*. Niki shares her tips for elevating your space and making it look like a place where you *want* to spend time—without spending tons of money—on her Instagram (@nikimcneill) and YouTube (@NikiMcNeillBrown) accounts. Finally, I spoke to Melissa Maker. She's an entrepreneur, author, and the person behind @CleanMySpace on social media; with nearly two million subscribers on YouTube and hundreds of thousands more across other social media platforms, Melissa is arguably the internet's foremost cleaning expert. What type of vacuum should you buy? How often should you clean your sheets? How do you keep a shower from getting scummy? Melissa offered answers for the cleaning questions you probably didn't even know to ask.

Here are the tips these experts offered for creating a visually appealing, functional, clean home:

1. Buy a good mattress.

If you've been carting around a stained futon mattress from place to place, it's time to let that go. Get yourself a grown-up bed. Think of how much time you'll spend in bed, between sleeping, watching movies, answering emails to your boss...you want it to be a comfortable place. But a mattress can be a serious investment.

Niki McNeill Brown offers a great tip: Specialty mattress firms offer specials on their products. Go to the store so you can try out different mattresses—you don't need to chance it with an online purchase. If you live near a mattress warehouse, you can get a great deal on a mattress someone has returned. Typically, mattresses will have a thirty-day return policy. If someone bought a mattress for $1,000, decided for some reason they didn't want it, and returned it, *you* can get that mattress for as much as 50 percent off. This method is a cool way to get a steal on a quality product. (The warehouse will sanitize and vacuum the mattress so you won't get stuck with something funky.) The lifespan of a mattress is about ten years; you'll have this for a while, so invest in something good. I always tell my kids that they're likely to change out their other furniture, but a mattress is something you keep for the long haul.

2. Remove visual clutter by purchasing items that contain storage.

When you walk into your apartment, where do you put your shoes? Do you have a designated spot, or are they scattered around the entrance—sloppy-looking and a trip hazard? Where do you store blankets, unopened mail, jewelry, cooking utensils...does each item have its place, or do you put things down at random and hope you'll be able to find them again when you need them?

To cut down on the visual clutter caused by stuff without a place to go, Niki recommends purchasing items that have storage capacity: for example, a chair or ottoman where you can store living room blankets. Having items stored in their proper place will make your space seem bigger; your home will feel more inviting and attractive, for both you and your guests. Consider your stuff and what you'd like easy access to. For instance, if you own a lot of board games and you'd like them to be easily accessible for when people come over, you could invest in a credenza or bookshelf—something in a central location—to house them.

3. Painting will give you the most "bang for your buck" when it comes to decorating.

The cheapest, most dramatic way to change the look and feel of a room is to paint it. Niki says the ceiling is also a canvas: you can paint a ceiling or add texture to it if you want a change. If you're renting, check your lease and see what it says about painting (landlords are usually okay with it, as long as you paint the room back to its original color before you move out).

Another cost-effective way to seriously change up a room is to add a rug. Niki says our eyes are drawn to these big canvases first: the walls, the ceiling, and the floor. A rug can add warmth and color to a room.

Pro tip: Many home improvement stores, such as Home Depot, will allow you to "test" a paint color before you buy it by uploading a photo of your room and then trying out different shades. You can also do this with some online rug retailers. In addition, AI can be your friend when you're decorating. There are lots of programs where you can describe the picture you have in mind for your space—the AI will show you a picture of it.

4. Follow your own design impulses rather than social media.

Niki said social media like TikTok and Instagram can present overwhelming options and opinions when it comes to decorating a space. Some looks become trends...but do you like them? You're not decorating your space for social media: you're decorating it for *you*. You get to live here. What do you like? If a trend speaks to you, emulate it. If not, don't worry about it. You can go to decor stores or flea markets and see what pieces stand out to you. What do you like about them? Your place doesn't need to look like a showroom, and you don't need to decorate it all at once. Gather items you like, piece by piece, until your home is a true reflection of you.

Niki described being a young adult as a "second adolescence." You're trying to figure out how to be in the world, outside of who you've been in your parents' home and then college. This period can be stressful. Your home, says Niki, should be a safe harbor you can come back to; a place where you feel at ease. If your home is going to be that safe space for you, it needs to *feel* like you. Follow your impulses; don't worry whether they're "trending" or not.

What do you need to know to take good care of your place? Fortunately, if you're renting, the answer is: not a lot. Your landlord should take care of most of the maintenance of your apartment. (Remember the last chapter: this is why it's important to rent from a professionally managed rental complex where landlords *have* to do things the right way.)

But there are a few basic maintenance things to know when the unexpected crops up, even if you're a long way from home ownership. Here are Jeff Thorman's expert tips:

1. Know where your electric, water, and gas shutoffs are. Know how to turn them off.

   Jeff said the two biggest emergencies people experience in their homes are fire and flood. These disasters can be cut off at the head if you know how to turn off your water, electricity, and/or gas.

   Jeff said if something goes wrong with a water valve, it's $3 or so to replace; if things flood, you've got a much bigger problem on your hands. Know where your water shutoff valve is. If you're unsure, you can ask the apartment manager to show it to you. That way, if there's an emergency and maintenance can't get there quickly, you can at least shut off the water supply and prevent further damage.

   For turning off your electricity, Jeff said the circuit breakers that control the flow of electricity don't need to be as "scary" as they appear. There's a metal plate on these circuit breakers that protects you. You won't get shocked as long as that metal plate is there. Let's say you need to turn off your power: If the switch is left, push it right. If it's right, push it left. The process really is that simple.

2. Make sure you have a fire extinguisher, carbon monoxide detector, and fire detector.

If your apartment doesn't have a fire extinguisher, carbon monoxide detector, and fire detector, you need to supply these things on your own. Jeff said this is especially true if you're living in an old house that's been converted into apartment units. Let's say you rent a basement apartment: if there is no fire detector in the basement, or it's not wired with other fire detectors throughout the house—that's a (potentially) *very* dangerous situation. Also, most fires originate in the kitchen; steps down to basement apartments are often right beside the kitchen. Is there an alternate entrance to the apartment? You need to check that *before* you sign your lease. If you're renting a unit in an old house, things may not be up to code safety-wise. (Once again; this is why the best practice is to rent from a *professionally managed* apartment complex where the operators have to do things safely and legally.) Make sure you have a carbon monoxide detector and fire detector and that they are wired correctly with other such units throughout the house or apartment complex. Note: Carbon monoxide detectors are especially important if you've got appliances that use natural gas. Also, check the batteries every six months.

Jeff said if you're renting, you don't need too many tools. However, there are a few he recommends everyone have. These include:

- Plunger
- Hammer for hanging pictures

- Measuring tape
- Multi-head screwdriver: you'll need this for putting together furniture
- Crescent wrench

…And that's it. If you're into tools, by all means get more. But a few basics will take you a long way.

Remember, though; if something goes wrong and you're not sure what to do, contact your apartment maintenance team *first*. This is why you're paying rent; so experts can be on hand when things get sticky.

SIDEBAR
CLEANING

After college, Melissa Maker wanted to start a business. She saw a need for a good cleaning business… but that was ridiculous, because Melissa *hated* cleaning. Which meant she needed to find efficient ways to do it. Nearly two decades later, Melissa is the creator of @ CleanMySpace, a YouTube channel dedicated to efficient and effective cleaning, and even wrote the book on cleaning (of the same name, *Clean My Space*). This accidental cleaning expert has tips on how to keep your space clean *enough*. As Melissa says, she aims for 60–70 percent clean on most days—no one's space is perfect, all the time. Here's how to walk that middle ground:

1. Clean your sheets once a week.
    A 2022 UK study found that 45 percent of single men said they don't wash their bed sheets for up to four months at a time, with

12 percent admitting they wash them when they remember—which could be even longer. Repeat after me: *yikes*[9].

Melissa said she can walk into someone's bedroom and immediately tell whether or not their sheets are dirty by scent. Think of your sheets, says Melissa, like T-shirts. They get sweaty. They collect dead skin cells and absorb body oils. A *lot* happens in your sheets; they need to be cleaned weekly. Have a spare pair of clean sheets; when you take off one set to wash, put on the other. Don't wait until someone comes into your bedroom and wrinkles their nose to think: "Hmm, maybe it's time to clean my sheets."

2. Clean your bathroom every other week.

Melissa said you don't need to spend hours at a time cleaning your bathroom; ten to fifteen minutes will suffice. A clean bathroom is especially important if you're having guests over. What makes for a clean bathroom? Be sure you: empty out the trashcan, wipe down the mirrors and counters, and clean the sink and toilets.

Melissa has an awesome hack that will keep your shower clean so you don't have to spend extra time scrubbing it: Keep a squee-

---

9 Saman Javed, "Almost half of UK's single men wash their bed sheets just once every four months, study finds," *The Independent*, April 28, 2022, https://www.the-independent.com/life-style/single-men-bed-sheets-four-months-wash-b2067438.html.

gee in your shower. Spend one or two minutes squeegee-ing after you finish showering. This will keep soap residue from mingling with calcium deposits and forming scum all over your shower. Squeegee, then ventilate the bathroom for at least thirty minutes after your shower and your shower will always stay clean.

3. Prevent a cleaning backup in kitchen; clean as you go throughout your week.

    The sink is a "bottleneck" in the kitchen, Melissa says; when it's full of dirty dishes, the mess spills over into other areas of your kitchen. Instead of allowing the bottleneck to form, clean as you go; rinse dirty dishes and put them straight into the dishwasher. Clear and wipe the sink and counters daily. Remove dishes from the dishwasher when they're done, so you can load the dishwasher up again and prevent junk from accumulating.

4. Vacuum and dust every day.

    The more you vacuum, the less you have to dust. Melissa says young adults should vacuum and sweep every day. She recommends investing in a high-quality vacuum; you can go to Consumer Reports or Wirecutter to see product reviews. A good vacuum can cost four figures; it may feel hard to justify that price. However, Melissa said cheaper vacuums that cost a couple hundred dollars are pretty much guaranteed to break in twelve to twenty-four months. Consider asking for this as a gift, or making a purchase on Black Friday or other big annual sales events.

5. Clean your cleaning appliances.

This is something you probably don't think about; every now and then you need to clean your cleaning appliances (think your dishwasher, laundry machine, and dryer). Melissa says to do this if you notice, for example, that the clothes you're getting out of the washing machine are still partially dirty or smelly.

6. Don't let your laundry sit.

If you let your laundry sit too long in the washer, it will get smelly and negate the wash those clothes just had. Take out your laundry and move it to the dryer as soon as it's done. Likewise, take your clothes out from the dryer quickly to prevent them from getting wrinkles. Separate your light and dark clothes to preserve the color of each when they're washed.

7. To declutter, keep your "hands full."

"Hands full" is a concept from the restaurant industry. If you're working in a restaurant, you have to stay busy so that the restaurant stays clean and people get served on time; rather than seeing you idly leaning against the counter, the manager always wants to see you with your "hands full," doing some task to keep the restaurant going.

You can apply the same concept to decluttering. Each time you're going from one room to another, keep your hands full; take items back to where they belong. This helps prevent the buildup of clutter. Clutter becomes a problem, says Melissa, when it's inhibiting how you do your work. Keep it from accumulating by getting in the habit of taking things back to where they go.

8. "OHIO"—only handle it once.

When you're doing a cleaning task, do *all* of it—and only handle it once. For example: groceries. Getting and putting away groceries involves several steps: cleaning out the fridge. Putting empty containers in the dishwasher. Unpacking the groceries. Storing the reusable grocery bags. Do all of this at the same time so you don't have random tasks hanging over your head; also, this approach will keep you from getting confused about what still needs to be done.

Here are Melissa's must-have products and cleaning solutions for keeping your space "clean enough":

PRODUCTS

1. High-quality vacuum
2. Microfiber cleaning cloths (These clean all surfaces, are reusable, and won't scratch your surfaces)

3. A sponge for cleaning the sink
4. Rubber gloves
5. Stepladder for hard-to-reach surfaces
6. Mop

CLEANING SOLUTIONS

1. All-purpose cleaner; or make your own with water and dish soap
2. Dish soap
3. Glass cleaner; or make your own with equal parts water and vinegar (However, don't spray screens with this solution! It will ruin your screen)
4. Toilet bowl cleaner
5. A scouring product, such as baking soda (*Scouring* means polishing something by removing dirt, grease, and other gunk from it)
6. Laundry detergent
7. Stain and enzyme remover
8. A disinfectant: for instance, Clorox wipes if someone in your house is sick and you want to keep the sickness from spreading

What is "clean enough" for you? As Melissa says, there is no set standard for cleaning. Like every other part of adulthood, your ideas of what is acceptable are informed by your upbringing and what feels good for you. Determine your "clean enough"—if you have a roommate, have open and honest conversations about your expectations. Recognize that your roommate's "clean enough" might be very different from yours—you'll have to determine together what your shared standard will be.

Yet even though there's no set standard for clean… wash your sheets. Aim for once a week—two times a month *at minimum*. Now you know.

THE "HEY, DAD" PARTING SHOTS

Furnishing and taking care of a space constitute some of the finer points of adulthood. You don't *have* to have a well-ordered apartment in order to survive; if you never hung a picture and your only filing system was a plastic organizing drawer left over from college, you'd be okay. And yet, we can do a little better than that. Assuming your home is someplace you'll spend a lot of time, you might as well arrange it how you like, know the basics of home maintenance, and keep it fresh and clean.

You're likely to own a home someday. Think of all this as practice for when your name is on the mortgage. Taking care of a space isn't an option when you're a homeowner, or something you do only when you think about it; it's an ongoing, everyday activity. You can handle it. Start small, right where you are.

TL;DR

Here are the "too long, didn't read" bullet points for everything we covered in this chapter:

- Buy a good mattress.

- Have a system for removing visual clutter. Buy furniture pieces with storage.
- Painting is the cheapest, most effective way to change a space.
- Know how to shut off the water, gas, and electric in your apartment.
- Be sure you have a fire extinguisher, fire detector, and carbon monoxide detector and make sure they're working properly every six months.
- You can make many cleaning solutions yourself with water, dish soap, and vinegar.
- Clean your sheets once a week.
- "Clean as you go" in the kitchen.
- Invest in a good-quality vacuum.
- Clean the appliances that clean *for* you, like your laundry machine and dishwasher.

CHAPTER 8

GET A CAR

How to buy and maintain your ride

My first car was a ten-year-old light blue 1981 BMW 320I. She was gorgeous, sporty...and also a money pit.

I loved the coolness factor of that car. The name meant something—my own BMW. She ran half of the time, but for the time the car was running, she was great. But she finally died—and then it was on to the next one.

My second car was an even dumber choice for an eighteen-year-old New Hampshire kid: a 1987 Chevy Camaro IROC-Z. It was a rear-wheel drive muscle car—not the best choice for New England's snowy winters. I was done with used cars; this car was brand new. It ran great...but the insurance cost as much as the monthly payment. (I had a "heavy right foot" and liked to drive fast, which resulted in lots of tickets, which led to higher insurance payments.) I hadn't taken insurance into account when I thought of purchasing the car; lo and behold, I couldn't afford the ride. I had to sell the car six months later and took a big loss. Talk about a heartbreak.

My early car misadventures taught me a valuable lesson: a car costs a lot more than the sticker price. Costs I hadn't considered for either car purchase: Insurance. Maintenance. Gas. Not to mention sales tax and registration on the vehicle. That's a lot of money to put into something that begins depreciating as soon as you drive it off the lot. Most cars don't get more valuable with time: they get *less* valuable, immediately. It doesn't make sense to pour lots of money into a car.

But sometimes, we do things that don't make sense. Buying a car, just like buying a house or making any other major purchase, evokes strong emotions and preferences. What does a car brand mean to you? Are you interested in "coolness," or do you prefer safety and reliability? Why are we attracted to some brands over others? It's all strangely personal. As a young man, I would have taken an unreliable Ferrari, Maserati, or Porsche over a more basic, reliable purchase any day. That's not to say it would have been a good decision...but I probably wouldn't have cared.

That is, until I had to sell the car (again) or trade it in. Let's assume you're not going to do what I did and buy and sell two cars in close succession. (There are much better places to park your money than in a car payment.) What do you need to know about buying a car and maintaining it? What kind of insurance do you need? What games do car salespeople play, and how can you come prepared for aggressive sales tactics—and still get what you want?

Let's start with the first step: buying a car. I spoke with Ray and Zach Shefska: on their YouTube channel, Ray and Zach, they discuss the ins and outs of car buying—and their conversations are as entertaining as they are educational. Ray worked in the retail automotive industry for forty-three years; Zach is the founder of a concierge car-buying service, CarEdge. Together, Ray and Zach help their audience learn the ropes of car buying. Here's what Ray and Zach think you need to know about purchasing a car:

1. Know your budget.

A car costs a lot more than the sticker price. Taxes and fees that go along with the purchase can tack on up to 10 percent to the overall price. Then you have insurance, which can cost $150–$200 (or more) a month for younger drivers. How much will you drive the car? You'll pay for filling up. The car will also need basic maintenance—changing oil, getting new tires every now and then, inspection, and so on—on top of any other more serious problems you might run into.

Each of these items should be factored into your budget. Ray and Zach recommend putting no more than 10 percent of your monthly income to your car. That includes everything: car payment, insurance, gas, maintenance. If you make $60,000 a year and are considering a car payment of $500 a month (10 percent of your gross monthly pay before deductions), think again; the car payment is just the beginning.

How much car can you afford? Zach and Ray say it's crucial for you to know that before beginning the car-buying process. Get pre-approved for a loan so you can be clear how much a car will truly cost you each month. There are two good reasons for this: First, a car loan from your local credit union will more than likely have a better interest rate than anything you'd get at the dealership. (Remember good interest and bad interest; the lower your interest rate on a loan, the more money you keep.)

Second, a loan pre-approval puts you in a better bargaining position with the dealership. You can tell the dealer you'll take their financing plan—*if* they can match the one you got on your pre-approved loan. Also, you'll be able to resist any upsells a dealer will try to lure you with. Say: "I'm approved for this amount and I'm not going over."

2. Do your research.

Ray and Zach said user-generated content, such as videos on YouTube, Instagram, and websites, can serve as a great starting point for your car research. How long before the car starts to experience significant problems? What type of gas mileage does it get? Does a certain make and model of car often have an issue with a major (expensive) component down the line? Do your best to know the true cost of ownership over time. An older sports car, for example, is going to be really expensive to insure and maintain (a lesson my young self learned the hard way). Narrow your choice down to your top three to five models. Your top consideration should always be cost, Ray and Zach advise. You want a car you can keep for the long haul, not something you'll have to sell back—at a loss—because you can't afford it.

If you've narrowed your search and know which makes and models you're interested in, you should have a general idea of the going price for that car: what's a good deal, what's average, and what's asking too much. Go into the dealer armed with this information. Zach and Ray say to know your "out-the-door cost," as in everything it will cost to get the car from the lot to your driveway. If the out-the-door cost isn't in line with your budget, be prepared to walk away.

Read that again: *be prepared to walk away* (more on why this makes you a powerful negotiator in #3).

3. Rent the car you're thinking of buying.

If you want to do as little as possible at the dealer (or skip it altogether and buy via an online service), rent the car you're thinking of buying rather than doing a test drive at the dealership. When you *do* go to the dealership, be prepared for the car dealer's sales tactics. The most powerful thing you can bring with you is a willingness to say no and walk away. A car dealer will often go back to "talk to their manager" during a negotiation. Ray said if they're a new salesperson, they really may be talking to their manager; if they're an old pro, they're definitely not. It's a BS stalling technique to keep you waiting and wondering what the salesperson and their manager are doing. Then, the salesperson will come back and say, "This is our absolute best price, and it's only good for today." If you know your budget going in, you can either take or leave that price. Note: If you're going to the dealer, go at the end of the month, end of the sales quarter, or end of the year when the salespeople are eager to hit their quotas—you'll cut down on the BS back and forth (more on that later).

Most people, said Ray, are conflict averse; they don't want to negotiate and will take the salesperson's word that they're getting the best price, most competitive interest rate, or whatever it may be. However, negotiation is a natural part of buying a car from a dealer. If you're purchasing from Carvana or another online retailer, you're paying extra for the privilege of *not* negotiating. You're not necessarily getting a better deal.

4. Get a pre-purchase inspection.

Ray and Zach are strong proponents of getting a pre-purchase inspection if you're buying a used vehicle, either from a dealership or an individual. This means that you take the car to a third-party inspector who doesn't have anything to do with the sale. Even if you're purchasing a used Honda from a Honda dealer, for example, you can ask for a pre-purchase inspection from a third-party mechanic (rather than the dealership mechanic). These inspections are only about a hundred bucks, and most reputable used-car dealers allow them. If the dealership does not allow a pre-purchase inspection, that's a red flag—walk away.

Ray and Zach say not to rely on the car's history as told by a service like Carfax. Carfax is only as good as the information it gets. If an auto shop worked on a car and didn't report it, a car can show up as having a clean report even if it was involved in an accident. It's worth it to take the car for a pre-purchase inspection so you have an accurate knowledge of what's going on with the car *right now*.

5. The best time to buy a new car is December.

Ray and Zach say the best time to buy a car is December. Manufacturers have sales goals they're trying to hit by the end of the year; they offer incentives to dealerships and consumers in the interest of hitting those goals. December is also a good time to buy used cars, according to Ray and Zach. The only *bad* time of year to buy a used car is tax-return time—the spring. People get their tax returns and want to spend them; demand for used cars spike, which makes the prices spike.

Hopefully, you make a good car purchase and get a reliable vehicle for a good price (even if it's not the coolest car on the block). Now what? How do you take care of it?

If there are any two people who know how to answer that question, they're Mike McDowell and Travis Peterson. Mike is a veteran driver of the NASCAR-cup series with some serious street cred; he's won the Daytona 500 and the Brickyard 200 as well as other races in Formula Sports and NASCAR Series. Travis, Mike's crew chief, is the crew chief at Front Row Motorsports; he's got a background in engineering and merged his love of racing and engineering as a race engineer at Roush Fenway Racing before joining Front Row Motorsports. Race car drivers are notoriously tough on cars: they accelerate fast, brake hard, and drive hundreds of miles at a stretch. Race car drivers have to take good care of their equipment if they're going to complete the race and win. Here is what Mike and Travis think you need to know about caring for your vehicle:

1. Know where your owner's manual is and how to get under your car's hood.

    Each car comes with an owner's manual. You should definitely have the manual if you got the car from a dealer; if you got it from an individual, check and see that you have it, or ask the seller for the manual specifically. Have your manual in an easy-to-access area of your car. If you have a problem, you can scan through the manual, find your issue, and be more knowledgeable about the help you need.

Also, know how to pop the hood of your car. This is a latch in the front of your car; you press a button in the car which opens the hood, move the latch aside, and raise the hood. (Be sure your car is *off* when you do this! If you have a key fob, be sure the car is all the way off, including the auxiliary.) Know where things are, like the oil, windshield-wiper fluid, and the battery.

2. If you're driving a long distance, do a pre-drive inspection.

This doesn't have to be anything too intense. Check your tires; is any lower than the others and in need of air? If so, what's the problem—is it something obvious, like a nail in the tire? Also, make sure there are no fluids under the car: in other words, that the car is not leaking fluids. (Different fluids that contribute to the functioning of your car: oil, coolant, power-steering fluid, brake fluid, transmission fluid, and windshield-wiper fluid.) Finally, adjust your seat and mirrors so you're comfortable and alert enough to drive a long way.

3. Know your car's vitals.

Just like a doctor checks your vitals when you go in for a check-up, you need to be aware of your car's vitals. These are the basics that, when working properly, allow your car to run: Tires. Gas. Oil. Know how to do the basic things, like put air in your tires and check your oil. Be sure you're servicing your car regularly by doing things like having your tires rotated and going in for regular oil changes. Keep a record of the maintenance activities you do for your car so you know when you're due for the next appointment. If you turn on your car and it's making a horrible sound...shut it off. When in doubt, shut the car off.

SIDEBAR
TIRES

The most important thing on your car is tires. As Mike and Travis say, tires connect your car to the road: they're what make your vehicle stop and go. To learn more about tire care and maintenance, I spoke with Jason Kelley.

Jason runs a tire store, Kelley Brothers Tire and Auto, that has been in his family for the last thirty years. He's the guy to call when there's something funky with your tires. Ever hit a nail in the road and find yourself rolling on your car's wheel? Or hear the "pop" as your tire explodes when you're doing 65 on the freeway?

I hope not. Those are dangerous situations (not to mention expensive). Whether or not you learn to change your own tires, Adulting 101 requires you to have a working knowledge of the basics. I asked Jason what you need to know about tires to stay safe on the road; here's what he had to say.

1. Know what the numbers on the outside of your tire mean.

Let's say you have these numbers: 255/55/17. The first number is the width of the tire in millimeters. A 255 is about 10 inches. The second number is the ratio: the height of your tire from the rim to the top of the tire (called the sidewall). If you have a 255/55, the sidewall is 55 percent of 255 millimeters. The last one is just the size of the wheel itself. In the US that hasn't converted to metric, which is why that is still measured in inches. Smaller tires are 14s, 15s, 16s; larger tires are 18s, 20s, 22s.

If you open up the driver's door in every US car, you'll see a little white-and-yellow placard. That tells you the standard size tire that should be on your car on the front and back wheels. For 90 percent of cars, the front wheels and back wheels should be the same size.

You can rotate those tires, which means moving the front tires to the back and the back tires to the front, so that the tires wear evenly. You can only do that if all your tires are the same size. Front tires wear out quicker than back tires, so that's why rotating is beneficial. Best practice is to rotate your tires every 5,000 miles, or when you go in for an oil change.

The placard on the door will also tell you what air pressure you should expect to run those tires at. Most of the tire-pressure warning lights are set at 35. If it gets below 35, your air pressure light will go off on your dashboard.

2. Know how to put air in your tires.

If your air-pressure light comes on, you may ruin the tire if you drive on it longer, said Jason. A tire that is under-inflated builds excess heat and becomes inefficient and dangerous; tires burst when they encounter too much hot air.

First, look and see which tire is low. Your dashboard light may tell you. If not, get out and do a walkaround and see if you can spot the problem. If you put air in the tire and then the light comes back on, you probably have a slow leak. If your air pressure is really low—anything in the 20s—stop driving. If it's a 15 or 20, don't drive at all; you'll damage the wheel if you do.

When you check air pressure in your tires, check the pressure in the spare, too. It's better to over-inflate than under-inflate. Tires can handle 45 or 50 psi (pounds per square inch) of air.

Just an FYI; when you unscrew the tire cap to inflate your tire, air will not leak out.

3. Try not to mix tire brands.

Jason said if you have three Michelin tires, you shouldn't get a Pirelli tire (or another brand) for the fourth. If you do mix brands, have the same brand on the front wheels or the same brand on the back wheels. As for how long tires last, Jason said it's not uncommon for people to get 60, 70, or even 80,000 miles out of a set of tires.

4. You can't mix gas and diesel, or vice versa.

It's the lesson my daughter learned on her road trip with her friend—the lesson she woke me from a perfectly good sleep to learn. You can't mix gas and diesel; gas engines and diesel engines are completely different. Gas stations can be confusing. Rec-90, ethanol, no ethanol...how do you choose the right fluid for your car? The key thing to know is if you have a gas engine, you can only put gas in it. If you have a diesel engine, you can only put diesel in it. You can, however, mix different grades of gasoline. At the gas station you usually have three options: 87 (the cheapest), 89, and 92. These are octane ratings; they refer to the fuel's ability to resist "knocking" or "pinging" during combustion. It's fine to put in 87 or 85 if you usually put in 89, for example. Just don't put in diesel. With oil, you need to be more careful; be sure you're giving your car the type of oil it requires. (It will tell you on the engine oil cap and in the manual.) However, if you're really low on oil, put in the type of oil you have on hand and drive the car to get serviced.

If you have to put in a fluid besides oil, best practice is to go to a shop. Take antifreeze; you can really mess up a car by putting in the wrong brand of antifreeze because this is manufacturer dependent. Don't chance that one on your own.

CHANGING YOUR CAR'S FLUIDS

Do you know when to change your car's fluids? If not, here's a quick-and-dirty guide:

- Oil: For synthetic oil, change every 5,000 to 10,000 miles. For conventional oil, change every 3,000 to 5,000 miles. If the oil level is low, change it immediately.
- Transmission fluid: For manual-transmission vehicles, change every 30,000 to 60,000 miles. For automatic-transmission vehicles, change every 60,000 to 100,000 miles.
- Brake fluid: Change every two years or 30,000 miles, whichever comes first.
- Radiator coolant: Change every two years or 30,000 miles.

5. Be careful when dealing with batteries.

Mike and Travis said that on newer cars, the battery is hard to get to. That's because the battery is part of an expensive computer and electrical system in the car; messing up the battery can mess up those, too. If you're doing anything battery-related on a newer car, it's best to take it to the dealership. If you need to jumpstart a battery on an old car, be sure you place the cables where they go: positive (red) with positive and negative (black) with negative. Once they're plugged in, don't let the cables arc or touch; you'll get zapped and ruin your whole day.

Sooner or later, you'll have this experience: you go to a maintenance shop for a quick oil change and the mechanic comes to you with another item on your car in need of fixing… for the cool price of $2,000. How do you know if they're telling the truth?

The best way to find a mechanic you trust is to talk to *people* you trust. Where do they get their cars serviced? As a secondary source of information, look at online reviews. You want to find a shop convenient to your location, staffed by people you trust, and build a relationship with the mechanics there. That way, when they inevitably say your car needs something, you'll know they're telling the truth.

SIDEBAR
INSURANCE

Don't forget that part of the overall cost of vehicle ownership is insurance. Your monthly insurance premium has to be a part of your car buying decision. Yet how exactly does car insurance work? Here, Mark Flockhart, the insurance expert who taught us about renter's insurance in chapter 6, offers his best guidance on how insurance works and getting the coverage you need.

1. Insurance is about protection, not just cost.

   When you pay your monthly car insurance premium, what exactly are you paying for? You're protecting yourself in the event of an emergency. But you're also covering medical expenses for other people you might be in an accident with. In a worst-case scenario: let's say you were texting and driving and got into an accident in which another motorist was killed. You only had $200,000 worth of insurance— but the costs of the accident outweighed that (financial costs and emotional costs). You or your parents—depending on the address on the insurance forms—could get sued by family members of the deceased driver; if you don't have the money, they could take assets from your parents, like their house or savings.

That's a worst-case scenario, but bear in mind that insurance protects *you* if there's an accident; it also pays for collision and accident coverage with other motorists, and it can pay for the medical bills of people in the car with you. How much risk do you want to take on? The more coverage you have, the higher your premium will be. Be smart—and also, be a safe driver.

2. Shop around for insurance or go through an independent broker.

    It can be overwhelming to shop for insurance and compare coverage and costs from different agencies. If you shop online, you'll get comparative costs for different agencies—at the cost of putting in your phone number, and then fielding dozens of calls for the next month. Mark recommends going with an independent broker who works with multiple agencies and can get you the best rates. Find someone to trust. If you need an insurance person, ask your parents or someone else who's been doing this a while who they recommend. Remember from the "Get a Place to Live" chapter—if you can bundle renters' and auto insurance, do. You'll get a better deal than if you purchased them separately.

3. Don't file a claim unless you have to.

The more claims you have on your insurance, the more your premiums will go up. If you can avoid filing a claim—as in, if you have a minor fender bender with limited damage or can fix the issue without going through insurance—do. For example, if you were backing up and hit a stationary car, leave a note with your contact information; hopefully you and the other driver will be able to resolve the situation without insurance. If both cars were moving and collided—either because you were at fault or the other driver was—then call the police. Then, call the insurance company. That is, after all, what you're paying for. Read the fine print in your plan regarding what they'll pay for if you have an emergency (for example—rental car? What's the process of getting that?). If you're unsure of whether or not to file a claim, call someone you trust and get their opinion.

Note: Moving violations, a.k.a. tickets, also have an impact on your premiums. Speeding, not coming to a complete stop at a stop sign, making an illegal turn...to take things back to Driver's Ed 101, it pays to be a safe driver and *not* do any of those things. (Another lesson my young self learned the hard way. Pour one out for my Chevy Camaro IROC and those insurance payments I couldn't afford.)

136

4. Understand the different types of coverage:

The different types of coverage in your insurance policy are:

- **Liability coverage:** Bodily injury liability pays costs if you injure someone else; property liability pays for damaged property.

- **Uninsured and underinsured motorist coverage:** This covers you and pays for your medical bills if you're hit by a driver who doesn't have insurance.

- **Comprehensive coverage:** Comprehensive coverage protects you in the event your car is damaged by hail, theft, vandalism, or fire.

- **Collision coverage:** This covers damage to your car if you're in an accident and have to get your car repaired.

- **Medical payments coverage:** Medical payments coverage pays for your medical bills in the event of an accident. Also, it covers medical payments for passengers in your vehicle or someone else who is driving your vehicle.

- **Personal injury protection:** This pays for your medical payments; it can also cover other costs incurred because of an accident, like lost income (only available in some states).

THE "HEY, DAD" PARTING SHOTS

Whether or not you've bought a car on your own, you will one day. Car buying, maintenance, insurance—it's all part of adulthood. Whether you like flashy, prestige vehicles like I did (RIP to my first BMW) or can't tell the difference between a Ford and a Ferrari...you can make an educated car-buying choice. You can take care of a car and have it for a long time. When you get a car that lasts you ten years or so, you simplify your life—you don't have to go through the car-buying process every year, and you don't waste money on something that depreciates in value.

You don't have to do it all on your own. Find a mechanic you trust. Same goes for an insurance broker. If you don't know where to look for those services, ask around. You'll be okay—as long as you don't put diesel in your gas engine.

TL;DR

Here are the "too long, didn't read" bullet points for everything we covered in this chapter:

- When car buying, know your budget.
- Get pre-approved for a loan so you know exactly what you can spend.
- Look to user-generated content online when researching cars. Know the true cost of ownership, now and ten years from now.
- The most powerful thing you bring with you into a car dealership is a willingness to say no and walk away.
- Ask for a pre-purchase inspection if you're buying a used car, whether from a dealer or an individual.

This should be performed by a third-party inspector who is not invested in the sale outcome.

- The best time to buy a new car is December. The *worst* time to buy a used car is tax-return season.
- Know how to get under the hood of your car and where your owner's manual is.
- If you're driving a long distance, do a pre-drive inspection. Make sure the tires are okay, the car is not leaking fluids, and you feel comfortable in the driver's seat.
- It's better to over-inflate than under-inflate your tires. If your tire psi is in the 20s or dips below 20, stop driving immediately.
- Don't put diesel in a gas engine, and don't put gas in a diesel engine.
- Be careful when dealing with batteries, but know how to jump them.
- Insurance is about covering you and anyone else you may be involved in an accident with. The higher the coverage, the higher your monthly payments. Consider how much risk you're willing to take on.
- Understand all the types of coverage on your policy. The types vary from state to state, and you can opt in or out of certain coverages.

CHAPTER 9

EVERYDAY MANNERS
AND ETIQUETTE

How to not embarrass yourself in public

The man kept pouring himself more wine.

We were at a dinner party. There were two couples in their twenties, one in their thirties, and one in their forties. If you haven't been part of such dinner parties yet, I hope you will be. Intergenerational gatherings are a great opportunity to make new friendships and learn from those in a different stage of life. I encourage my kids to stay teachable in these moments. Observe. How are others around you handling themselves? What do you find attractive or off-putting about the ways they're behaving or treating others?

At this party, the man in his thirties kept pouring himself more wine—to the point where it was uncomfortable for everyone else. Rather than serving his partner or those around him, he kept filling up his own glass, even if others around were empty. This man gave off the impression that he was both sloppy (it wasn't long before the wine caught up with him) and selfish. It wasn't a good look, and it left a bad taste in everyone's mouth.

I wondered: Why didn't his parents didn't teach him better? That's what this chapter is all about.

Consider; what are the criteria that make for a pleasant, functioning adult? What are the cheat codes for being a good person whom others like to be around and who contributes meaningfully to society?

That depends on who you ask. Everyone has their own "rules" for life, and they're heavily influenced by the environment in which you grew up. For instance, my mom has a saying: "Weddings are optional, funerals are not." It's an encapsulation of her personal belief system, and it was encoded in me at a young age. Her reasoning: at weddings, everyone's in a good mood. Who doesn't want to dress up, eat free food, and watch two people on their happy day?

Funerals, on the other hand, are easy to say no to. They can be uncomfortable. By attending a funeral, we put ourselves in a potentially awkward situation: What if we say the wrong thing and cause *more* pain to the grieving person? What if tears catch us off guard and we become a blubbering mess in front of people who've never seen that side of us? What if it's all just too depressing? *Go anyway*: that's what my mom taught me. If you're close enough to the person to *know* about the funeral, you should make an appearance. The grieving person or family will never forget your presence. Just being there is an act of solidarity, encouragement, and love.

But other people weren't raised with that instruction. I spoke to experts in being a good person, manners, and etiquette for this section—one etiquette expert said they sometimes skip funerals (but always send flowers or a card). My point is, there's no one rubric for how to adult "right." What we think is correct is informed primarily by our family of origin. Media we consume, our friends, and life experiences all add to the data set in our brains that make up our portrait of a "functioning adult"; however, the initial data set is given to us by the people who raise us.

Which criteria has the most weight? Maybe you have a credit score of 850—but you can't see your bedroom floor because it's buried under piles of dirty clothes. Maybe you know how to change a tire, but you like to start fights in the comments section of strangers' posts. You may excel in some areas of adulting but lag behind the baseline in others. And that's assuming there *is* a baseline; if such a thing exists, where is it, and how do we measure our relation to it?

In this chapter, I wanted to explore how to excel in some of the finer points of everyday adulting. Most important to this mission is being a good person. At the end of the day, that's what parents want: for their kids to grow up into good people who contribute to society. We don't care if our kids are the best athletes, make the most money, or if they become high-ranking politicians…but we do want them to treat people well and leave the world a better place. I spoke to a philosophy professor who researches Kant's moral philosophy, critical thinking, disagreement, and the nature of philosophy; I wanted his take on what makes a person "good," and how we can all strive to be better than we are today. Yet good people can still make asses of themselves in public—I don't want you to do that. So, I spoke with experts in the realm of manners and etiquette (and I learned the difference between the two). Knowing proper manners and etiquette does not make you a boring stiff with a stick up your you-know-what; rather, knowledge of social graces enables you to feel comfortable in new situations, make others around you comfortable, and get ahead in life and business.

We'll cover many of the basics on how to be a good person and what to do in different social situations. But if you have specific questions about what to do, etiquette-wise, when you're faced with new circumstances, the internet is your friend. We can't cover every scenario here; thankfully, social media exists. Research the specific situation you're preparing for so you don't end up ordering a sloppy joe with chili fries when you're meeting your significant other's parents for the first time, or "ordering an appetizer for the table" at a business dinner—and getting a bowl of soup for yourself. (Yes, that's a real thing a former intern in my company did.) Remember: even if you make a faux pas out in the real world, you don't have to stew and beat yourself up. Apologize when necessary and chalk the experience up to learning. Nobody masters this stuff right away; we all become more gracious and comfortable in the world with time. Let this section be your "leg up."

WHAT MAKES A GOOD PERSON?

This is what I wanted to know when I spoke with Robert Gressis, a professor at California State University, Northridge. Robert referenced Aristotle, who said that a good human is someone who can "flourish." This involves strengthening virtues—such as kindness, generosity, and honesty—so that you become a "virtuous" person. Robert said one of his personal turnoffs is when people are dogmatic: they have strong, unyielding opinions on things they (usually) haven't spent much time thinking about.

Does our idea of what makes a good human change as we get older? Robert says yes: as we get older, we tend to value certain virtues more than others. There are no "ethical prodigies." This means none of us are born knowing right from wrong or with a finely tuned sense of what to do in morally gray areas.

USE SOCIAL MEDIA WITH CAUTION

Robert said we overestimate the importance of what we're doing when we post on social media, and that people are less polarized than they appear to be online. According to Robert most social media posting is an attempt to gain status, no matter how much we may disguise our motives from ourselves. Lying to ourselves about our motives is not good for our personal growth.

Excessive social media use has also been shown to make people unhappier. Not only does it make you unhappier; too much social media can derail your career (even your life). Your digital trail follows you forever. There's the philosophical case against too much social media (that it fosters division among people and stunts your emotional growth) and the practical one (it makes you unhappier and can harm your life and career prospects). Both are good reasons to get out in the real world and talk to people face-to-face.

BE KIND OR TELL THE TRUTH?

There's such a thing as "radical honesty." If someone asks you what you think of their skirt and you hate it, you tell them so. On the other end is lying; telling someone the skirt looks great. Which one is better?

Robert said that for honest people, lying feels bad. They won't thrive in situations where people are encouraged to lie— for instance, to get ahead in business. If you're in a situation like that, get out. For more everyday situations where lying is not the norm (one exception being poker, where you're *supposed* to lie), telling the truth and being kind don't have to be in opposition. For instance: you don't have to tell your friend you hate their skirt and they should burn it. You could say something like: "I think your green skirt suits you better than that one." Reading between the lines, your friend may get the message that you don't like the skirt. Or you could just tell them: "The skirt is not my favorite, but if you feel good in it you should wear it." You're expressing concern for the person over regard for your own opinion; you're deploying empathy, kindness, and thoughtfulness. The Golden Rule is as good a rule of thumb as any when determining what to say. Would I want someone to say this to me or treat me this way? If you run interpersonal communication through that filter, others will enjoy being around you and you'll feel good about your relationships.

Also, learn to master these words: "I'm sorry." Learn to say them without a "but" chaser (as in, "I'm sorry, but that color *is* ugly on you"). Stay humble and learn to admit when you're wrong. Life is not just about the relationships you make; it's about the relationships you *keep*. If you know how to truly say "I'm sorry" when you're wrong, you'll keep your relationships for a long, long time.

HOW TO TELL RIGHT FROM WRONG

Robert said most of the time, people know right from wrong. If they're having difficulty over a decision, it's because doing the right thing feels hard. Even people who commit crimes have a sense of right and wrong that isn't far off from the moral sense of someone who *doesn't* commit crimes; the reason people break the law is, in large part, due to their environment. They're in a setting in which everyone around them is making moral compromises; for example, cheating on the final exam of a notoriously hard professor or applying for fraudulent loans as a way to generate quick cash. Robert said it's not often that we're *really* confused. Here again, the Golden Rule comes into play. Would you want someone to do this thing to you? If you were the professor, how would you feel if a large portion of the class cheated? What is the institution to which you're applying for the fraudulent loan, and what happens if they catch on? We can justify immoral behavior in many different ways—but at the end of the day, we know right from wrong. When we're in situations where those around us are upholding a high moral standard, we have an easier time doing the right thing—even when it's hard.

Yet even if we know right from wrong, we can still slip up in social situations if we're unsure of how we should comport ourselves. That's why I spoke with two experts in manners and etiquette: first of all, to learn the difference between the two concepts—and secondly, to provide tips and best practices for putting your best foot forward whatever scenario you find yourself in.

WHAT'S THE DIFFERENCE BETWEEN MANNERS AND ETIQUETTE?

Thomas P. Farley is known as "Mister Manners" and "America's Trusted Etiquette Expert." He regularly makes appearances on the NBC *Today* show, *Inside Edition*, and other programs across the United States to provide viewers advice on how to handle themselves in various social situations. I liked how he made the distinction between manners and etiquette: Manners, Thomas said, are treating people with kindness and respect. When you have good manners, people feel better after they've interacted with you. Etiquette, on the other hand, is a social roadmap that guides us through specific business and social situations. For example: at a Christian wedding, guests of the bride sit on the left side of the auditorium and guests of the groom sit on the right. That's etiquette. Jacqueline Whitmore, business etiquette expert and author of *Business Class; Etiquette Essentials for Success at Work*, made a similar distinction: She said manners are *how* you treat someone. Etiquette is *knowing* how to treat someone.

Let's say you're unsure of the etiquette in a certain situation. For instance: you're invited to a party and the dress code is "Miami chic." What is that supposed to mean?

Both Jacqueline and Thomas offered simple advice for this scenario: just ask. Call the party organizer and ask what they will be wearing. This goes for any situation in which you're not sure of the etiquette: call someone who will tell you honestly, and/or someone you don't mind looking clueless in front of. There are also YouTube videos covering every conceivable etiquette situation. Do your homework if you feel unsure.

Thomas said even if *you* know proper etiquette and someone else does not, don't make anyone feel "less than" for not knowing the rules. Here is where your manners come into play. Basically, no one likes a snob—don't be one.

Here are some things to remember as you step into the world, best foot forward:

1. First impressions are everything.

According to Jacqueline, it only takes thirty-three milliseconds for someone to form a first impression of you. First impressions are hugely important. But what elements contribute to a first impression? Here are a few:

- **Handshake:** Your handshake needs to be *firm*. A weak handshake may signify to the other person that you're not serious, that your mind is somewhere else, or that you don't respect them. It also conveys a lack of self-confidence. A firm handshake, on the other hand, is a sign of respect. It reveals how you feel about the other person.

  A note to the guys: if you're meeting your partner's dad, the dad *will* judge you by your handshake. He just will. If you want to make a good impression, accept this and prepare.

- **What you wear:** You don't have to be dressed to the nines every time you step out of your door. However, you do need to be put together. Are you dressed for the occasion (whatever the occasion is)? Are your clothes ripped? Stained? Both Jacqueline and Thomas recommend getting a full-length mirror so you can check your appearance from head to toe before stepping out. This is especially important if you're entering a scenario where your appearance and first impression really count, such as a job interview.

- **Phone etiquette:** Let's say you're meeting a date for the first time: your date approaches you at the restaurant and your head is buried in your phone. Or you meet your significant other's parents, look up briefly from your phone to say "hi"—and then you continue text conversations with your friends all night. Neither of those are a good look.

It's common courtesy to silence your phone and give whomever you're with your full attention. Anything less will signify disrespect. Bonus: if you're fully present for your interactions with other people, you'll enjoy those interactions more and deepen your appreciation for the people in your life. You'll be happier if you put the phone down—and others will appreciate your full, undivided attention.

2. Social etiquette and business etiquette are different.

Both Jacqueline and Thomas said that business etiquette is gender neutral. For instance, it may be perceived as condescending and offensive for a man to soften his handshake when interacting with a female colleague (though a bone-crushing handshake wouldn't be appropriate, either). In a client situation, the business representative pays for the client—regardless of either party's gender. Men can and should hold the door for women, and vice versa.

Social etiquette still falls more solidly along traditional gender lines. For instance, Thomas said studies show many women still expect men to pick up the check on a date—particularly a first date. Socially, it would be appropriate for a man to pull out a woman's chair at dinner; this would be inappropriate and unusual in a business setting. Etiquette guidelines exist to ensure everyone feels comfortable in social situations—particularly situations that are unfamiliar. Let that be your yardstick when determining when and how to follow the rules.

A note on business dinners: if you're invited to a business dinner, remember that you're not there to eat a great meal—you're there to work. Be guided by your boss. Be polite, but don't blabber out of turn. Don't order something sloppy or difficult to eat (save the ramen noodles for a night out with friends). Don't get drunk. Use your manners; ask questions of your dinner partners, be genuinely interested in their responses, and be willing to share about yourself in turn as appropriate (no oversharing). Be an asset to the business—not a liability.

3. A handwritten thank-you note will make you stand out.

If you write a handwritten thank-you note, you *will* stand out. Jacqueline believes going to the effort of writing a thank-you note—whether you're thanking an interviewer, someone who gave you a gift, a new connection who gave you valuable career advice—is always worth it. She even recommends every young person have their own personal stationery and an area dedicated to writing and sending letters. This is definitely old-fashioned—which is why it's a valuable practice. So few people take the time to handwrite and mail thank-you letters that someone who does is guaranteed to get noticed.

As Thomas points out, you cannot go wrong by sending a handwritten letter. (Who could possibly be offended by such a thoughtful gesture?). Think of all the useless items you get in the mail: credit card offers, magazines you never subscribed to, bills, and more. A handwritten note is like a breath of fresh air. Thomas recommends that if you go for an in-person interview, bring a stamped envelope with you. Immediately following the interview, find a coffee shop or other place to sit and write a thank-you note, mailing it from the same zip code where the interview took place. Like Jacqueline, Thomas says writing thank-you notes should be a matter of course: make the practice routine and simple.

4. Master the art of the introduction.

Thomas said he enjoys being the connector between two people. This is a powerful role. When you're introducing two people you believe will benefit from knowing one another, you never know what might happen. Those people could begin dating, get married, start a business, become best friends—the possibilities are endless. Connecting people can spark beautiful possibilities for those people; they'll also feel goodwill toward *you*. Not to get too woo-woo, but you're energetically opening the door to have others connect *you* with interesting people who will add to your life. When you're serving as a connector, give people something to go on: introduce people by telling each person something interesting about the other.

When you're introducing *yourself*, go for "memorable." Craft a one-liner that opens the door for further conversation. For instance: let's say you work in hospitality. The hotel that employs you is the preferred hotel for several major league baseball players during the training season. Rather than saying "I'm Derek, and I work in hotel administration," you can say, "I'm Derek, and I once overnighted a baseball player's lucky rosary beads from the Dominican Republic." I don't know about you, but if I heard that line, I'd have a lot of follow-up questions. That's what the one-line introduction is meant to do: start a conversation. Do this with new people you meet and you'll (a) stick out in the person's mind, and (b) enjoy your interactions more. That's a win for everyone.

THE "HEY, DAD" PARTING SHOTS

We all want to be good people. We want to be remembered. We want people to, as Thomas Farley put it, feel better for having interacted with us. That's what having good manners and proper etiquette are all about—not about following an arbitrary set of "rules" to fit into exclusive clubs or judging people who don't know the rules.

In young adulthood, you'll find yourself in many situations where you're learning new etiquette rules. For instance: What are the guidelines for buying someone a wedding gift? Or: What's the correct amount to tip the hotel cleaning staff? How do you work a table at a business dinner? Remember: there's a YouTube video for just about anything. If you mess up, don't worry: everyone's got a story of a moment they made a cringe-worthy social gaffe. Whatever the particulars of the story, that person never made the mistake again. Mistakes are how you learn—no matter how embarrassing it is now, you'll laugh about it in thirty years. Trust me.

TL;DR

Here are the "too long, didn't read" bullet points for everything we covered in this chapter:

- When you get down to it, you know the difference between right and wrong. Put yourself in scenarios where doing the right thing is encouraged.
- Be kind, tell the truth. You can do both.

EVERYDAY MANNERS AND ETIQUETTE

- Manners are how you treat someone; etiquette is *knowing* how to treat someone.
- Business etiquette is gender neutral; social etiquette still falls along more traditional gender lines.
- First impressions are *everything*. To make a good first impression, have a firm handshake.
- Not sure of the etiquette in a certain situation? Look it up online or ask someone who will tell you the truth without judgment.
- Handwritten thank-you notes make you stand out—that's a good thing.
- Introduce other people to each other; they'll like you and you'll open the door for powerful, synchronistic introductions for yourself.
- Master your "one-liner" for when you introduce yourself—open the door for further conversation.

CHAPTER 10

TRAVEL

Amazing experiences you can afford

Some of my most stressful "Hey, Dad" moments come when my kids are traveling.

Once, one of my kids called me from the airport to let me know they missed their flight. That was a head-scratcher. How could they have missed it? We'd arrived at the airport well in advance of the boarding time.

"I went to gate D4, just like I was supposed to," said my kid.

I had their flight information and knew the gate was *not* D4. "Why'd you do that? You were supposed to board at E4."

"Oh," said my kid on the other end of the line. I could tell they were thinking. "It's a Delta flight. I thought I was supposed to go to 'D' for 'Delta.'"

Caught between annoyance and the urge to burst out laughing, I just shook my head. "Bet you won't make that mistake again."

They never have (and in fairness, prior to that moment I'd always been the one to lead my kids through the airport). Still, my blood pressure goes up when my kids travel across the globe, even though they're young adults now and mostly able to handle themselves. Whether you're a seasoned traveler or exploring the world on your own for the first time, spending some of your hard-earned money—there's a lot to know about *how* to travel. The *why* of travel is personal: every person has their own reason for exploring (or not) and things they hope to get from the experience. Personally, I think traveling is one of the best uses of your time and money. The world is an amazing place, full of amazing people: Why not see those places and get to know those people while you can? Traveling gives you an education like none other and experiences you'll remember forever. It deepens your understanding of the world and (hopefully) your appreciation for how people everywhere are different, yet basically the same at our core.

But that's just my opinion. Your reasons for globe-trotting (or country-trotting, or state-trotting) are as good as mine. Wherever you want to go, start plotting how you'll get there and what you'll do. You may catch the travel bug—and not the kind that keeps you holed up over the toilet bowl in your hotel room. I'm talking about the *good* kind, the one that compels you to explore. Fascinating destinations are more within reach than you may imagine.

I interviewed Doug Barnard to learn what it takes to travel to some seriously far-flung places most US tourists don't even think of visiting (think Iraq, Bangladesh, and Pakistan, just to name a few). Doug is a YouTuber who also leads group and private trips to destinations off the beaten path. If he can lead strangers through Iraq, he can help you get to your work conference in Atlanta. Here's what Doug had to say about how to choose your destination and get the most out of your trip:

1. Choose destinations commensurate with your level of experience.

For your first international trip, you probably don't want to go someplace with limited tourism infrastructure. Iraq, Pakistan, Bangladesh...the places on Doug's bucket list are often developing countries without much support for tourists. Doug recommends going someplace more traveled if you're foraying into international travel. A tourist in Paris is going to have a much easier time than a tourist in Iraq. If you would like to go to less-traveled corners of the globe, as Doug does, consider going with a tour group. A good tour leader should have connections with locals, which will grant you access to experiences you wouldn't be able to get otherwise.

Not every travel destination requires only a passport. Some also require tourist visas and vaccinations. Visit your country's State Department website to view travel guidelines to the specific country you're interested in visiting. For more obscure destinations, Doug also recommends connecting online with travelers who have visited that location. He said Facebook groups and Reddit threads are a good place to do this.

2. Look to user-generated content for travel destination ideas.

Doug grew up only hearing negative things about Iraq. During his entire childhood and young adult years, the US was at war with Iraq; Iraq wasn't talked about outside of the conflict. Doug was interested in geopolitics and exploring places outside of the news headlines associated with that location—so when Iraq opened to tourism, Doug immediately knew he wanted to visit and see for himself what the country is like. Now, he visits frequently and even leads tour groups there.

Where do you want to go? Follow your interests and curiosities, as Doug did. Doug also recommends user-generated traveler content for picking your next destination. Explore social media and travel blogs and see what sparks your imagination. Once you choose a destination, delve more into the particulars of your visit. Doug said the neighborhood you stay in is a key part of your travel experience, so make sure you stay in a well-reviewed area.

Note: If price is your number one concern, you may want to search for deals and *then* look for destinations, rather than choosing the destination first. We'll cover that later in this chapter.

3. Double and triple check your documents. Give yourself plenty of time at the airport.

What are the official forms you need to visit your destination? Keep a checklist—especially for documents such as passports, visas, and other official forms required to enter a country. Also, make sure you've got a checklist for your general packing and you've accounted for differences you'll encounter once you reach your destination—for example, power adapters that enable you to use your electrical devices abroad. (Note: In the "Oh, Crap!" section of this book, we'll cover what devices you need to have handy for various situations.)

Give yourself plenty of time at the airport. Don't try to squeeze in an extra twenty minutes in a city before heading back home—you run the risk of long security lines and missed flights. (And remember, if you're traveling internationally, you'll have to go through customs as well.) You don't want that kind of stress at the beginning or end of your trip. Get to the airport early; be sure you've got the right location for your departing gate (remember, those can change).

Doug said depending on where you are, countries have different requirements on whether or not you should have your passport on you at all times. In Western Europe, for example, you may not need to carry your passport and can leave it in the hotel safe. (Read that again: the hotel *safe*. Not your luggage.) In countries where you *do* need your passport at all times—you'll know it. Doug says it's a good idea to have a photocopy of your passport and to have that on you when you're out and about.

Other good ideas: always carrying at least $100 in US cash for emergencies. Doug recommends *not* taking out local currency before you arrive in the country. Anything you buy or exchange in the arrivals hall of an airport is much more expensive than what you'd pay in the city center, which is what Doug recommends doing. For example: Doug often buys SIM cards with data in the city center rather than at the airport. Doug also recommends frequent travelers have a checking account that rebates ATM fees all around the world so you can draw out cash in the local currency without heavy fees.

4. Be aware of your surroundings and watch out for scammers.

Doug said to keep a "healthy dose of skepticism" when you travel, especially to avoid being ripped off. For instance: if you step out of the airport and suddenly have dozens of drivers approaching you competing for your business, be wary. They may sell you on one price to get you in the car, and then jack it up closer to your destination. If you're somewhere where there are lots of tourists, there are potentially lots of scammers, too. If someone approaches saying, "Hello, my friend!"—and this is someone you've never seen before—be wary. That person might dupe you into taking your picture in front of the Pyramids—and then demand payment for the "service." In those situations, Doug says it's best to say no politely but firmly and keep on walking. If you're traveling with a guide, they can help you sidestep some of the nonsense.

Safety-wise, be sure someone knows where you are at all times. Have access to the internet (this is where purchasing a SIM card with data comes in handy). Share your travel itinerary with someone beforehand...for instance, your parents. We like to know what you're up to, preferably before the day of travel. Also, buy travel insurance. Doug said travel insurance offers great coverage and is generally pretty cheap (roughly $100 for up to two weeks of travel). Doug recommends travel insurance that covers flight/travel cancellation, *and* insurance that covers you if you have medical or evacuation needs. If you're in a developing country and need medical attention, Doug recommends going to the nearest private-pay hospital. Hotel staff may also be able to recommend a good care facility, or you can ask a local. When all else fails, you can always Google hospitals in your area.

5. Try local foods, but exercise caution.

Eating local food is a great way to get to know a place and its culture better. Street food can be delicious—but exercise caution when you're choosing a meal, especially in developing countries. Doug says if you notice a lot of people eating from a particular vendor, the food is probably safe to eat. A food cart with no lines and meat that's been baking in the sun for six hours? Probably not a good call. Avoid fruits and vegetables—in other words, food that's been washed with water. (If the fruit can be peeled, like oranges or bananas, it's fine.) This means avoiding garnishes and food that would go into a salad. Drink bottled water; avoid ice in your drinks. You can always ask a vendor to leave off a particular garnish or ask if the food has been prepared with filtered water. If the answer is no, choose something else. Best practice is to use bottled water for any activity in which water enters your mouth, such as brushing your teeth.

Street food is not the only food that can make you sick. Just because something is served in a brick-and-mortar restaurant doesn't mean it's "safe." There's not a 100 percent foolproof way to avoid getting sick when traveling in developing countries, but you can apply the same criteria you use for street foods when evaluating brick-and-mortar establishments. Are there many local people dining at this restaurant? If so, it's a safer bet.

6. Be humble and open.

Travel is a great way to learn more about the world and gain an appreciation for other cultures and ways of life. Be humble, Doug says. Travel with an open mind. Be ready to have your preconceptions challenged. The last thing you want is to be the "ignorant American" who comes in and expects people to serve you. Be flexible; understand that things won't always go according to plan, and that's okay. Learn a few key phrases in the local language. Even if you're not a fluent speaker, using phrases like "please" and "thank you" signify respect to the locals where you're traveling. Remember: people live here; you're just a guest. Act as if you're a guest in someone's home. This attitude will open the door to rich, rewarding experiences and new friendships.

SIDEBAR
PASSPORTS, REAL ID, AND GLOBAL ENTRY

You probably know that a passport is essential if you want to leave the country. But do you have one? What is the process of getting one? And what about other forms of identification when you travel?

If you're unfamiliar with how to obtain a passport, Real ID, or Global Entry (or even with what these terms mean), this is for *you*:

1. **Passports:** A passport is good for ten years. However, if you're within six months of the expiration date of your passport, you can't travel out of country. Also, it can take some time to get a passport, roughly six to eight weeks. If you think you'll be traveling out of the country in the near future, be sure you have a passport, you know where it is, and that it's up to date. Not sure if you'll be traveling abroad? Get a passport anyway. You never know when you'll need it!

   To obtain a passport, go to the State Department website (travel.state.gov). Note: There are online "companies" that try to trick unsuspecting travelers into giving up personal data under the guise of "rushing" your passport application. Don't fall for it; make sure you're visiting an official government website, which ends in .gov. There you can learn what forms you need and where your nearest passport office is.

2. **Real ID:** The Real ID Act was created in 2005 in response to the 9/11 terrorist attacks. Basically, it's a way to ensure that each state adopts and implements uniform standards for issuing identification. By May 7, 2025, all IDs shown at TSA must be Real ID compliant. You'll know if your driver's license is Real ID compliant because it has a gold star on it. Be sure you check what Real ID–compliant licenses look like for your state; if yours is not compliant, request a replacement.

3. **Global Entry:** Global Entry is a way for low-risk travelers to quickly make their way through customs upon entry into the United States. If you've got Global Entry, a machine simply takes a picture of your face to verify it's you—and then you get to skip the (sometimes hours-long) customs line. Take note; the process to be approved for Global Entry is rigorous. You have to apply, have a background check, and pass an in-person interview. The application fee is $120 (as of October 2024), and if you're approved, Global Entry includes TSA Pre-check and lasts for five years. (TSA Pre-check means you can move through security quickly; you don't have to remove coats, shoes, laptops from

your bag, or belts). If you travel internationally frequently, Global Entry is definitely worth
looking into.

"Okay," you may be thinking, "maybe travel is rewarding—
but it's *expensive*. Must be nice for some folks to travel around
the world, but I'm on a budget. Is travel open to me, too?"

Yes, it is. Scott Keyes is the founder of Going, formerly
known as Scott's Cheap Flights, a travel platform with more
than two million members. Scott, a journalist by trade, had
heard of people getting cheap international flights. "How are
they doing it?" he wondered. Then, "Why can't I do it too?"
Scott went down an internet rabbit hole searching for good
deals on flights, and in 2013, he got the best deal of his life:
a $130 round-trip airfare from New York City to Milan. The
flight was so cheap, it gave Scott the opportunity to spend his
money on other things on his vacation, like traveling to Lake
Como, taking in an AC Milan soccer match, and hiking the
Cinque Terre. That trip changed the ballgame for Scott. Since
then, he's turned his interest in budget travel into a service that
helps average people travel the world for seriously discounted
prices. Here's what Scott had to say about finding the best travel
deals:

1. **Take advantage of your flexible schedule.**

    Scott described the way people usually look
    for flights: Decide where you want to go. Decide
    when you want to go. Look for flights and book the
    ticket. This method is the least likely to get you a
    good deal on your ticket.

For young adult travelers who are time rich but (often) cash poor, flexibility pays off. You can flip the traditional flight search model on its head by making affordability your primary search criteria. When you search in this way, you first look to see: From my city's airport, where can I get cheap flights? (Understand that the destinations available to you will change by the day.) Let's say you live in New York: you see that from LaGuardia Airport, you can get a $350 roundtrip ticket to Miami, a $450 roundtrip ticket to Paris, and a $300 roundtrip ticket to Colombia. Ask yourself: Which destination interests me the most? Then, see which dates are available and work with your schedule. By setting "price" as your top priority when booking flights, you open yourself to a range of travel possibilities and new experiences.

2. **Book your ticket directly with the airline.**

It's a good idea to search for flights via third-party websites that compare different rates from different airlines. That way you can find the best deal: for instance, you may find that an American Airlines flight is $100 cheaper than a Delta flight, which is information you wouldn't have if you only searched on Delta. Once you've found your flight, however, book directly with the airline. Booking with the airline affords you better protection than booking with a third-party website. There's a federal regulation that affords you the ability to cancel your flight within twenty-four hours of booking—which only applies if you book directly through the airline. If there's a change to your flight and you booked with a third-party website, that website may or may not let you know about the change.

3. **Use credit cards—responsibly—to earn airline miles.**

What's the deal with earning flight benefits with credit cards, anyway? Scott used to be a skeptic. Using a credit card to get free flights: it seemed too good to be true, like there had to be some catch. Scott changed his tune when, as a college student, he wanted to visit a friend doing a Fulbright scholarship in the Galapagos Islands. The flight was $1,600, an amount of cash he didn't have. However, Scott did have 100,000 airline miles from flying to and from college: a roundtrip ticket to the Galapagos cost 30,000 miles. Scott was amazed: he'd earned a free ticket to the Galapagos with zero effort.

If you're a responsible user of credit, airline miles accrued via credit card usage can be a great way to visit destinations on your bucket list. "Responsible credit user" means you don't carry a balance on your credit card: each month, pay your balance in full so you're not subject to interest charges. Credit cards that offer miles rewards offer the reward *after* you spend a certain amount: for instance, $3,000 in the first six months of use. Before you sign up for the card to get the reward, be sure you can meet the minimum spend without buying a lot of expensive gadgets or stuff you wouldn't normally buy. Also, beware of fees. If you open one card (or several), know that these cards carry yearly fees, usually in amounts of $95 all the way up to $650 or more. Make sure you account for the yearly fee when you're considering the overall cost/benefit of a new credit card. Don't fall into the trap of opening a bunch of new credit cards for the miles bonuses and then paying hundreds in unanticipated fees.

A free way to earn airline miles: when you book a flight on a particular airline, sign up for their rewards program. Be sure you get credit for the flights you've already paid for with cash.

4. **Optimize your buying time for the best deals on flights.**

Airfare is the most volatile thing we routinely purchase. It's not uncommon to see a flight for $500 one day, then $300 the next day, and then $1,300 the next day. While the prices of hotels, Airbnbs, rental cars, and other big-ticket travel purchases remain relatively stable by comparison, airline fares have massive swings in price.

You're more likely to find the best deal, Scott says, if you book your flight during the "Goldilocks" window (think of Goldilocks eating the bowl of porridge that is not too hot and not too cold, but "just right"). For domestic flights during "off-peak" times, the Goldilocks window is one to three months in advance; for peak times, three to six months in advance. For international flights during off-peak times, book two to eight months in advance; for peak times, book four to ten months in advance. "Peak" times include: Christmas, New Year's, middle of summer, St. Patrick's Day in Dublin...you get the idea.

Scott says, "Today's cheap flight is tomorrow's expensive flight." If you see a deal that's "too good to be true," go ahead and book it. (Remember that if you book directly with the airline, you can cancel the purchase within twenty-four hours if you need to.) Sometimes airlines publish "mistake fares." For instance, the ticket Scott purchased from New York to Milan for $130 was probably a mistake fare—it's likely the airline forgot to add a zero to the price. Usually, airlines will honor the mistake fares because it's bad business to give a group of travelers a great price and then suddenly cancel. If you book what you believe is a mistake fare, sit tight. Wait at least a week to see if you hear from the airline that they're planning to cancel the fare. If you can still log on and see your ticket, you're good to go.

5. **Don't buy refundable tickets.**
    Scott said he's never booked a "refundable" ticket in his life. These tickets are much more expensive—and they're unnecessary. Most main economy tickets on major airlines are already refundable.

If you book a ticket for June 7 and then need to change your departure date for June 9, you can call the airline and do that. If the June 9 departure ticket is cheaper—let's say $180, when the original ticket you booked was $200—the airline will give you $20 in credit. (If the second ticket costs more, then you've got to cover the difference.) The rules for basic economy are different. In some instances, you may be able to cancel for half credit—often, you won't be able to get any credit at all. However, basic economy prices are much cheaper on the front end. How sure are you of your travel dates? Are they likely to change? Your answers to those questions will inform your buying decisions.

Bear in mind: if the airline cancels or significantly changes your flight, you're entitled to a full cash refund by federal law.

6. **Find the travel deals in oversold flights.**

When Scott was in his early twenties, he would sit by the gate agent waiting for an announcement saying the flight was oversold and the airline was looking for people to give up their seat for travel credit. Scott would jump on these opportunities—with a stipulation. He would give up his seat *if* he got the maximum travel credit offered to other passengers, or "best as last." Gate agents will ask for volunteers willing to give up their seats on oversold flights for $200 in travel credit...then $400, then $600, then $800 (or in increments of their choosing). Scott says to remember this is a negotiation. If you have the flexibility, jump on these deals—with the stipulation that you want the "best as last" credit.

7. Missed a flight or a connection? Don't freak out.

If you've missed a connecting flight due to the airline—for instance, there was a mechanical issue, or the pilot overslept—the airline is obligated to provide you with hotel, meal, and transportation vouchers. You can go to the Department of Transportation's website and head to the Airline Customer Service Dashboard:[10] there you'll find what each airline promises you as a traveler if your flight is delayed or canceled.

What happens if you miss your flight and it's *your* fault? Don't assume, "I missed my flight, there's no point in going to the airport." Scott said often, the airline can put you on the next flight, free of charge. This is a favor to you, not something you're entitled to—so don't count on it. Still, it never hurts to ask, so be polite and friendly. Best practice is to get to the airport well ahead of your departure time. Relax; read a book; people watch. Being slightly bored ahead of your departure is a lot better than racing through the airport trying to get on the plane before the doors close.

---

10 "Airline Customer Service Dashboard," U.S. Department of Transportation, updated May 31, 2024, accessed November 1, 2024, https://www.transportation.gov/airconsumer/airline-customer-service-dashboard.

THE "HEY, DAD" PARTING SHOTS

Here's the truth: traveling will get more complicated when you're older. When you have a mortgage, kids, school schedules, and/or a partner's schedule to navigate, getting away becomes a lot more difficult. (Definitely possible—just more difficult.) *Now* is a great time to see parts of the world you've always dreamt of. Go in with an open mind; be respectful of other cultures and remember that you're the guest—they live here. Be flexible and humble. Focus less on getting the perfect shot for social media and more on meeting interesting people and learning about the world. Nothing will give you a better education than traveling.

TL;DR

Here are the "too long, didn't read" bullet points for everything we covered in this chapter:

- Travel. Make the effort. It's worth it.
- If it's your first time traveling abroad, go somewhere with a lot of tourism infrastructure.
- If you plan to travel in an area with less tourism infrastructure, going with a guide can smooth your travel experience and get you access to one-of-a-kind experiences.
- Be sure you know which documents you'll need to travel—passport, visa, etc.—and double and triple check that you have them.
- Get to the airport well ahead of your departure time, especially if you have to go through customs.
- Have cash for emergencies, at least $100 in USD.

- Don't drink the water in developing countries: use bottled water. Also: don't drink beverages with ice or eat fruit or vegetables that have been washed with local water.
- Always communicate your travel itinerary with someone.
- You can search for tickets on third-party websites, but book your airline ticket directly with the airline.
- For the best deals on domestic flights, book one to three months in advance. For best deals on international flights, book two to eight months in advance. For peak travel times, book four to six months in advance (domestic) or four to ten months in advance (international).
- If the airline cancels your flight, you're entitled to a full cash refund. Also: if you miss your connection and it's the airline's fault, they're obligated to give you vouchers for lodging, food, and transportation.

CHAPTER 11

"OH, CRAP!"

How to deal with emergencies

If I get a text from one of my kids, I think: "Great—I'll text back when I can."

If I get a call, I think: "Hmm. Wonder why they didn't text?"

If I get a *double* call, I think: "*Oh no.*"

Most parents fear the double call (not as much as we fear the middle-of-the-night call, but we still fear it). Phone calls from my kids come at all hours of the day; usually, when I'm sitting down to dinner with a client or about to have a serious business discussion. My "normal" business hours are about 7:30 to 10:00 p.m., and during that time frame I field phone calls from my kids on all subjects—a problem with a question on someone's college homework, someone's bored at work, someone's got a suspicious charge on a credit card and doesn't know how to handle it, and so on. But everything stops for the double call.

When I answer the double call, I usually expect a scene on the other end of the line. Somebody's in distress because something has gone badly wrong; could be that one kid has a pet who is scarily sick, could be that another is broken down on the side of the freeway. I've got to calm myself first in those situations. I know I won't be good to anyone if I lose my head (also if I say, "Calm down!" which has never, in the history of time, helped anyone calm down). My job as the dad is to take a deep breath, tap into a calm state, and try to transmit that energy over the phone.

Truth is, it can be unnerving to deal with emergencies on your own. Up to this point, your folks/caregiver have fielded all the emergencies: flat tires, power outages, ER visits, et cetera. When *you're* the one making those decisions—should I call an ambulance? Where are the backup batteries? How high a fever is *too* high?—it's a different ballgame. If in the past you've freaked out in the face of the unexpected, you're not the only one. But you've got this.

Life happens. Emergencies pop up; for you, me, and everyone else. When they crop up for you, the key thing is to *stay calm*. Pretend I'm your dad on the phone, talking you through it. You can't make good choices if you're frantic. If you're panicked, you stand a good chance of interfering with the scene and making a bad situation even worse. No matter how bad things look, you can make the choice not to freak out.

As my kids have gotten older, they've become better at this. You will, too. Age gives you the wisdom to see that not every "emergency" is a five-alarm fire; some things are just hassles. Inconvenient and unexpected, but not life or death. Coping with emergencies begins with having a strong mindset. To learn more about how to deal when life goes sideways, I spoke with Joel Lambert.

Joel spent a career in the SEAL teams and is the former star of the reality television show *Manhunt*, in which he would be dropped off someplace with a survival kit and a designated extraction point; on the show, Joel had to make his way to the extraction point—and deal with the whims of nature—before being found by people who were "hunting" him. Joel is an expert on being prepared for anything and maintaining a level head, no matter what surprises life brings. Here's his advice for coping with emergencies with a healthy mindset:

1. Make the decision to endure.

Joel recounted his experience in Navy SEALs training. There, he trained with several people who had been college athletes in their physical prime; other trainees referred to them as "gazelles," able to perform nearly impossible physical feats. However, some in this group were completely defeated by BUD/S training. "BUD/S" stands for "Basic Underwater Demolition/ SEAL," and it consists of three phases: physical conditioning (seven weeks), combat diving (seven weeks), and land warfare (seven weeks). Joel said there is some element of BUD/S that defeats everyone; the challenge lies in seeing how you will react to it. How do you respond when you're faced with something you can't overcome, or something you *perceive* you can't overcome? Many of the elite athletes couldn't handle the rigor or mental defeat; they would drop out of training. Someone with a stronger mindset but less physical prowess is in a better condition than an Olympic-level athlete.

Joel also recounted the story of a group of four siblings who were the only survivors of a plane that crash-landed in the Amazon in Colombia. With no technology, the siblings walked for forty days—and made it out. They followed the river and just kept going. What gave these children the stamina? Without parents or other adults, how did they find the mental fortitude to keep walking? But something within the children propelled them forward. They had no resources or technological support—and yet they made it out.

A strong mindset will take you far, says Joel—much farther than any physical assets or resources money can buy.

2. Break down difficult tasks into small increments.

Joel spoke of his time in BUD/S training—how after the first week, he had a real "oh, crap" moment. How was he going to make it through all of the twenty-plus weeks of training? He couldn't conceive of all those weeks at once; he had to break the time frame into time chunks that felt manageable. "I'll just make it through this first phase; then I'll decide what to do." "I'll make it through this second phase; then I'll decide." When something is too overwhelming, break it into smaller parts. Joel mentioned the siblings walking through the Amazon and the importance of designating "little victories" to keep your spirit strong, as in: "I'll just walk for one more day." Then that victory is achieved, and you set *another* small goal and achieve *one more* small victory—and you keep on going. The tougher the situation you're facing, the smaller the time increments; you can do anything, says Joel, for three more seconds. If you need to break up time into three-second intervals, do. Do whatever you need to brace yourself for the long haul—specifically, not *viewing* it as a long haul but as something to endure for only a few seconds more.

3. Calm is a superpower.

When we feel threatened, our bodies know. You've probably heard of "fight, flight, or freeze." Our bodies respond when we're in those situations; our eyes dilate to take in more light. We get surges of adrenaline. We breathe quicker, which floods our bodies with oxygen. All of these responses, harnessed, can make us unstoppable. The key is to use them *for* us rather than *against* us—and our ability to do that lies in our ability to stay calm. Calm is a superpower, says Joel. Panicking in an emergency will help nothing; in fact, panicking will likely lead you to make dumb, dangerous decisions. Take a deep breath and maintain your commitment to staying calm.

4. "Get off the X."

In a combat situation where you're setting up an ambush for the enemy, the point at which the trap deploys is called the "X," said Joel. Joel was trained to engage the enemy—and then to "get off the X" as quickly as possible. This means to remove yourself from the dangerous situation, then assess what needs to be done. You can't make a clear decision in the line of fire.

When *you* find yourself in a dangerous situation (bad street, dark alley, etc.), get off the X. Look around for a safe place; remove yourself from direct danger. Stop, look, and listen—then, make your next move.

5. Know the Rule of Threes.

Let's hope you're never in a situation where you have to survive on your own in the Amazon rainforest. But if you are—remember the Rule of Threes: you can survive for three hours without shelter, three days without water, and three weeks without food.

This sets up an order of operations for you; your first order of business is to create shelter for your physical body so you'll be shielded from the elements. Then, find your water source. Finally, focus on procuring food. Animal instinct may kick in and tell you: "I have to find food—lots of it—*now*." Yet that is incorrect, said Joel; shelter comes first. Put your needs in their correct order (shelter, water, food) and better your chances for survival.

6. Have emergency supplies on hand.

Joel recommends having emergency supplies ready: on your person, in your car, and in your home. For your car, Joel recommends bottles of water, solar tire inflators, a tool that enables you to cut through seatbelts and windows if the electrical system of your car goes down, and a few MREs (meals ready-to-eat). He said that in certain situations, like snowstorms, people make the mistake of leaving their car and going for help; the car provides shelter, so leaving puts you at greater risk. For the home, Joel recommends having two to six weeks' worth of an emergency food stash and several cases of water. Joel carries a Garmin inReach, which is a tool that allows for satellite messaging should the communication system go down.

Yet the most important tool you can have in an emergency, says Joel, is a strong mindset. No matter what situation you're facing, make the decision to stay calm, endure, and figure it out.

Many emergency situations people face are self-made. Jack Raia, an EMT and content creator on TikTok with nearly 900K followers, spends his nights and weekends saving people. Jack helps people in life-or-death situations every day of the week, whether they've overdosed on drugs or have sustained injuries from alcohol-fueled barfights. How do you avoid these situations, or help if you find yourself a bystander while a friend or stranger is experiencing a crisis? Here are Jack's best tips:

1. **Pace yourself with alcohol consumption.**

    Jack works a lot of music festivals. He's often been in the medical tent with someone who drank far too much; now they feel terrible, aren't enjoying the music festival (for which they paid a lot of money), are in fights with friends over their alcohol consumption...they've created a lot of problems for themselves, Jack says, because they treated drinking like it was a race. Jack said no one thinks they're going to be the person blackout drunk in a medical tent—yet someone always is. Pace yourself with your alcohol consumption (or even better, rave sober).

    Jack said people who consume drugs at music festivals (or anywhere, really) are taking a huge gamble; they'll either have a terrible trip and ruin their night out, *or* they'll have a great time. The problem with having a great time; the person who ingests a certain cocktail of drugs and enjoys it will, next time, want to consume *at least* that same amount of drugs. Increasing your drug intake with each night out puts you at greater risk of having a seriously bad outcome (obviously)—not to mention the risk of exposing yourself to fentanyl, which is in everything now, says Jack. The wisest choice is to not consume drugs at all. Yet taking drugs when there's a chance those drugs contain fentanyl is extremely dangerous—at least purchase a test kit to make sure anything you consume does not contain fentanyl.

2. **Be naloxone trained.**

There are a few things the average person can do to assist in the event of an emergency, says Jack. The first are to learn life-saving techniques such as CPR, the Heimlich maneuver, and how to apply a tourniquet to stop bleeding. The second is to carry Narcan and know how and when to administer it. Narcan is the brand name of naloxone, which reverses the effects of opioids; if someone overdoses, Narcan can bring them back. It is not a "fix all" for every kind of overdose, only opioid overdose. Understanding the signs and symptoms of an opioid overdose is important. Jack said Narcan comes in the form of a nasal spray and is simple to administer. Jack works with a nonprofit called End Overdose11 that offers a course on how and when to administer Narcan; the nonprofit also distributes Narcan and sells fentanyl test strips (you can get five for five bucks). In addition, many firehouses distribute Narcan for free.

Finally, keep a basic first aid kit on hand (in your apartment, car, or both) to treat minor injuries.

3. **Call 911.**

Even if you're well prepared to give first-responder treatment to someone experiencing an emergency, call 911. If someone is drunk or expe-

---

11   End Overdose, https://endoverdose.net/.

riencing an overdose and in danger of choking or aspirating, first move them onto their side so their airway is clear. Then, call 911. Jack said sometimes people are afraid to do this, especially if they've been taking drugs—they're afraid they will be arrested for illegal consumption. However, if you are in need of treatment, HIPAA laws protect you in this situation as an EMT or nurse is not allowed to share your information with anyone not involved in your care. This means that if you tell an EMT you are on illegal drugs, that EMT is not allowed to share that with police officers. HIPAA is not what protects the bystander or friend who calls. Jack said Good Samaritan laws (which vary from state to state) would likely protect you in this situation; these laws state that since you are helping in an emergency, you are not subject to prosecution for illegal activity. Don't be afraid to call 911; get help sooner rather than later. It's important to note that despite what you are experiencing, if at any time you feel your life is in danger, do not hesitate to call 911 or seek out the nearest emergency room.

4. **Exercise caution with legal drugs and medications.**

Jack said they have seen an uptick in calls for cannabis use since it became legal. Jack lives in New York, where cannabis has been legal since 2021. No one has died from a cannabis overdose—yet cannabis can still have scary effects. Jack said he's responded to calls in which someone has taken an edible (cannabis is *much* more potent when it's digested rather than inhaled via smoke) and the person is now deeply physical uncomfortable, having a paranoid reaction, or some combination of the two. Neither of those are situations you want.

Also, Jack said to be wary of over-the-counter medications in your medicine cabinet. People use the labels "aspirin," "ibuprofen," and "Tylenol," as if the drugs are interchangeable—yet they're not. Aspirin is an anti-platelet aggregate which keeps platelets from sticking together; it's given to someone experiencing chest pain in order to prevent blood clots from getting bigger. Ibuprofen and Advil are analgesics, meant to reduce pain and inflammation—those are your best bets for reducing a headache, says Jack. Tylenol contains the active ingredient of acetaminophen; it has analgesic properties but is also meant for fever reduction. Tylenol is a good choice if you have the flu or flu-like symptoms. However, acetaminophen when taken with alcohol can mess up your liver. Don't take Tylenol when you've been drinking. For that matter, excess drinking coupled with any OTC medicine, even an analgesic without acetaminophen, can damage your stomach lining. (But if you're regularly getting drunk and relying on OTC medicines to curb your hangover…you already have a problem beyond your eventual stomach lining/liver degradation. Seek help.)

5. **Go to the ER when you need to.**

The ER shouldn't be your first option when you're facing a health situation, especially given how expensive it can be (even with insurance). If you're bleeding, can you stop the bleeding yourself? If so, bandage yourself up and go to urgent care if you need to. If not—time to go to the ER.

Also, go to the ER if you have a fever of 103 or higher. Jack said that with high fevers, the danger exponentially increases with each degree. A 102 fever is different than a 103, a 103 is *very* different than a 104...and so on. If your fever is 103 or higher, don't chance it; get yourself to an emergency room by any means necessary.

SIDEBAR
AUTO EMERGENCIES

Odds are, you'll be in a car accident at some point in your life (if you haven't been already). Hopefully it will be nothing more serious than bumping into another car in a parking lot. However, whether you experience a parking lot bump or a major accident that totals your car, there are protocols to follow to a.) ensure your safety, and b.) help you take care of your ride. I spoke with William (Bill) Van Tassel, PhD, who manages AAA's national driver training programs; he's responsible for teaching driving safety to *millions* of customers through the oldest and largest automobile association in the US (AAA has over sixty million members and has been around for over 120 years). Here's what Bill had to say about how to handle an auto emergency.

1. **Inspect your car before you drive and be prepared.**

   Bill echoed Mike McDowell and Travis Peterson, the NASCAR driver and crew chief, on the value of inspecting your car before you hit the road. Be sure your tires are fully inflated, you have enough oil, and that your car is not leaking fluids. Also, be sure your car is stocked with emergency-preparedness items in case you have a breakdown. Bill has in his car: jumper cables, a wrench to get tire lug nuts loose, a flashlight, extra batteries, a charging cord for a cell phone, and warm clothes (if you're driving in cold weather). Bill also recommends having a membership in an auto club, like AAA or another group. Then, when you have an emergency need, help is only a phone call away.

2. **Know how to jump a car and change a tire.**

   Bill said knowing how to change a tire, check your oil, and jump a car all come under the umbrella of "responsible vehicle ownership." Know how to do these things before you need to; practice basic auto maintenance in a non-emergency situation. (If your car is a newer model and has a wheel lock, be sure you have the wheel lock key in your car—without it, you can't change your tire). Get someone to show you the ropes, then practice. You'll be well prepared to help yourself—or someone else—in the event of an auto emergency.

3. **Move the car to a safe distance from oncoming traffic.**

In the event you are in an accident, says Bill, move the car as far away from other moving vehicles as you can. Pull over onto a shoulder; if you can get behind a guardrail, do that. If you have other riders in the car, check on them. Is everyone all right? Once you've assessed that no one is in serious danger, assess the impact of the accident on the car. What's the severity of the damage? Do you need to get the police involved?

Document the scene; take pictures with your phone. If there's another person involved, exchange contact information so you can report any relevant information to your insurance provider. (Information to exchange includes: name and number, driver's license number, license plate, insurance company and policy number, and make, model, and year of car.) If the police have been called, they will walk you through this process; they will take photos and ask questions in an attempt to determine who is at fault.

The most important thing is to make sure everyone is safe. If someone is injured, try not to move them until emergency services arrive—

unless you must because there is danger of being hit by oncoming cars, or fire. If you're in a car pileup—as in, you weren't one of the two cars that initially collided, but you got caught in the crash and you're okay physically—take the initiative to call 911 on behalf of the other motorists (and yourself). Regardless of the severity of the crash, when you're back home and in a safe situation, write down your recollection of everything that's happened. Do this while your memories are fresh. Nerves get rattled in auto accidents, and stories can change. To be prepared for dealings with insurance (and possibly law enforcement), write down your experiences.

4. **Stay calm.**

No one ever plans to be in a fender bender. Accidents can heighten your emotional state; there's the initial rush of fear and adrenaline caused by the accident itself, and then anxiety and frustration in the aftermath. Taking pictures, swapping information, dealing with police, waiting on the phone with your auto insurance—all of it takes time that's already been mentally allocated elsewhere. Stay calm. Growing frustrated will not help you. Take deep breaths. Accept, said Bill, that "this is my new priority for the day." All of that stuff you planned to do will still be there later, waiting for you. An accident feels like a major hassle and inconvenience, yet it's an experience to which almost everyone can relate. Stuff happens. That job interview you were headed to, the $500 you'll now have to come up with to pay your car-insurance deductible—none of that is important. What's important is your safety. Explain your situation to whomever you need to, and trust that things will work out.

Also: if you're on the other end of the line helping someone else through *their* emergency, stay calm. No matter how freaked out you feel internally, realize that no one will be helped by your panic. (Maybe this one is more for the parents and guardians.)

THE "HEY, DAD" PARTING SHOTS

In life, things won't always go according to plan. Every time you respond to emergencies with centeredness and calm, you gain another notch in your "adulting" belt. Maturity lies in knowing the degree to which you can make a bad situation worse by your actions—and then not doing that. Real adults—the kind you and I want to be like when we grow up—retain their center.

How can you do that? Joel Lambert meditates for an hour every day. Remember Dr. Lisa Miller, way back in the "Get a Plan" chapter at the beginning of this book? She advocates listening to the Universe—tuning in to guidance that, she says, is always available. If you do this on a regular basis, that sense of calm won't leave you, even when crap hits the fan. Living from a centered place when life is calm will help you respond appropriately when it's not.

You can prepare for certain situations, but life loves to throw the unexpected at us. Tend to your mindset above all else. Build resilience. Give yourself credit for the minor emergencies you handle. You've come through hard things before, without your world falling apart; there's no need for it to fall apart *this* time. Trust that whatever life throws your way…you got this.

TL;DR

Here are the "too long, didn't read" bullet points for everything we covered in this chapter:

- A strong mindset is the most important asset you can have in an emergency.
- Calm is a superpower.
- "Get off the X"—when you're in a dangerous situation, get out of imminent danger and assess your next move.
- Remember the Rule of Threes: you can survive three hours without shelter, three days without water, and three weeks without food.
- It's a good idea to keep emergency supplies on hand, both in your house and in your car.
- Call 911. Even if you're engaging in illegal activity (like using drugs), call 911 if someone needs it; you'll be protected under Good Samaritan laws.
- If at any time you feel your life is in danger, do not hesitate to call 911 or seek out the nearest emergency room.

- Go to the ER if you're bleeding and you can't stop it, or you have a fever of 103 or higher.
- Inspect your car before you drive it. Carry emergency supplies.
- If you're in an accident, move so you're safe from oncoming traffic. First check to see if everyone in the car is all right. Then, exchange information with the other driver (if it's a two-person collision).
- Stay calm. Accidents and emergencies happen.

CONCLUSION

My cell phone buzzed in my pocket. I looked at my watch: 8:00 p.m. After work hours, which meant it must be—

I pulled out the phone and saw one of my kids' names light up the screen.

Wonder why they didn't text? I pressed "answer."

"Hey, Dad."

"Hi." I paused. "What's wrong? What do you need?"

"Actually Dad, things are pretty great," said my adult child.

Was there a shoe hovering somewhere, about to crash-land on my head?

"They are?"

"Yeah, they are, Dad," my kid, now a full-fledged young adult, replied. "My friends and I are planning a trip over New Year's, and I'm pretty excited about it. I've got a great mentor at work...."

My grown kid went on for a few minutes, telling me about all the things they were looking forward to. I asked a few questions, but mostly I nodded and smiled...and gradually forgot my fear that I was about to be clobbered by a sneaker.

"...anyway, Dad, what's new with you? How are you doing?"

For the next fifteen minutes, my adult child and I connected: just talking about our lives and expressing our love and appreciation for one another. I hung up, so grateful for how well my kids were turning out.

And then the alarm clock went off and I woke up from my dream.

Okay, that phone call didn't happen. I made it up. But it *could* happen.

That's the kind of phone call I daydream about—and granted, now that my kids are getting further into adulthood, I'm noticing an uptick in non-emergency phone calls. As parents, all we ever want is for our kids to be okay. We understand that they *won't* be okay all the time—that's called "life." However, we want to know that our kids' good days outweigh the bad, that they have the tools they need to make the best of any situation, and that they're figuring stuff out and having fun as they go. Personally, I don't care whether or not my kids have the most degrees, or make the most money, or get promoted the fastest. I care about whether or not they're good people. I care about their relationships. I care about whether they're making decisions that will lead to their most fulfilling experience of life.

Regardless of where you are in your adulting journey, I hope this book has helped you do that. I hope you'll refer back to it often as you face new adulting scenarios. Even though I've attempted to make this book a "manual" on how to adult... no such manual exists. There are certain rites of passage every person making the transition from dependent to independent must face: getting a job, finding a place to live, figuring out how to keep that place clean, and so on. But I can't know your exact life situation. You'll face your own challenges based on your circumstances and your choices, and no manual could ever give you all the answers for how to react and what to do. Such a book would be twenty feet thick.

The good news: you don't *need* all the answers. You've got intuition and reason. Hopefully, you've got a supportive parenting figure—or absent that, a solid mentor on whom you can lean for advice. Right now, you're garnering experiences which in twenty years will add up to "wisdom." Everything you've been through in the past contributes to that wisdom, too. You're not starting from zero. Wherever you were when you picked up this book, you were already on your way to a fulfilling and fun life. I hope this book has taken you one step closer.

Remember that you've lived through all your worst days up to this point. Whatever you'll face in the future—no matter how bad things get or how badly you screw up—things can be set right. You don't have to know everything. (No one does!) Rather, find people you can lean on and who remind you that *you got this*, no matter what you're facing. Adulting may seem scary—and it can be—but it's a lot of fun, too. With your independence you can create new opportunities for yourself. You can choose to be unconstrained by limits that held you back in the past. You can change your mind. You can change careers, or cities, or decide you want to go back to school, or sell all your possessions and move to a beach in Costa Rica—*whatever you want*. The freedom is dizzying.

Not every choice will be the right one *for you*, but with some experimentation you can feel your way into your best-fit path, like a mountain climber searching for the ledge or crevice that will give her the best purchase on the rock. You scale upward, one movement at a time. Then you get to the top, and the view makes your jaw drop. You enjoy it for a few blissful moments. And then you see another mountain in the distance....

That's life, too; there's always another mountain to climb. The challenges make life exciting. We didn't come here just to sit around and one day die—we came to try some stuff. Just know that there's never any place of "arrival" where you reach *true* adulthood. (I'm still waiting to feel like a real adult.) Since we never truly arrive, we may as well enjoy ourselves—all the way up one mountain, then the next, then the next.

Here's to making the climb. You've got this!